Massachusetts'
BICYCLE
TRAILS

An American Bike Trails Publication

Massachusetts'
Bicycle Trails

Published by American Bike Trails

Created by   Ray Hoven
Designed & Illustrated by   Mary C. Rumpsa

Table of Contents

Table of Contents (continued)

How to Use This Book

This book provides a comprehensive, easy-to use reference to the many off-road trails throughout Massachusetts. It contains over 50 detailed trails maps. Trails in this book are organized alphabetically. The back of the book provides indexes in alphabetical sequence of all the trails illustrated, plus separate listings by leisure and mountain biking, and cross references by city to trail and county to trail. The trail maps include such helpful features as locations and access, trail facilities, and nearby communities.

Trail Related Terms

Length	Expressed in miles one way. Round trip mileage is normally indicated for loops.
Effort Levels	**Easy** – Physical exertion is not strenuous. Climbs and descents as well as technical obstacles are more minimal. Recommended for beginners.
	Moderate – Physical exertion is not excessive. Climbs and descents can be challenging. Expect some technical obstacles.
	Difficult – Physical exertion is demanding. Climbs and descents require good riding skills. Trail surface may be sandy, loose rock, soft or wet.
Directions	Describes by way of directions and distances, how to get to the trail areas from roads and nearby communities.
Map	Illustrative representation of a geographic area, such as a state, section, forest, park or trail complex.
DNR	Department of Natural Resources
DOT	Department of Transportation

Bicycle Safety

Bicycling offers many rewards, among them a physically fit body and a pleasant means of transportation. But the sport has its hazards, which can lead to serious accidents and injuries. We have provided rules, facts and tips that can help minimize the dangers of bicycling while you're having fun.

Choose The Right Bicycle

Adults and children should ride bicycles with frames small enough to be straddled easily with both feet flat on the ground, and with handlebars that can be easily reached with elbows bent. Oversize bikes make it difficult to ride comfortably and maintain control. Likewise, don't buy a large bike for a child to grow into--smaller is safer.

Learn To Ride The Safe Way

When learning to ride a bike, let a little air out of the tires, and practice steering and balancing by "scootering" around with both feet on the ground and the seat as low as possible. The "fly-or-fall" method-where someone runs alongside the bicycle and then lets go-can result in injuries.

Training wheels don't work, since the rider can't learn to balance until the wheels come of. They can be used with a timid rider, but the child still will have to learn to ride without them. Once the rider can balance and pedal (without training wheels), raise the seat so that the rider's leg is almost straight at the bottom of the pedal stroke.

Children seldom appreciate the dangers and hazards of city cycling. Make sure they understand the traffic laws before letting them onto the road.

Use This Important Equipment

Headlight A working headlight and rear reflector are required for night riding in some states. Side reflectors do not make the rider visible to drivers on cross streets.

Safety seat for children under 40 lbs. Make sure the seat is mounted firmly over the rear wheel of the bike, and does not wobble when going downhill at high speed. Make sure the child will not slide down while riding. The carrier should also have a device to keep the child's feet from getting into the spokes.

Package rack Racks are inexpensive, and they let the rider steer with both hands and keep packages out of the spokes.

Get A Bike That Works With You

Skilled riders who use their bikes often for exercise or transport should consider buying multi-geared bikes, which increase efficiency while minimizing stress on the body. (These bikes may not be appropriate for young or unskilled riders, who may concentrate more on the gears than on the road.) The goal is to keep the pedals turning at a rate of 60-90 RPM. Using the higher gears while pedaling slowly is hard on the knees, and is slower and more tiring than the efficient pedaling on the experienced cyclist. Have a safe trip!

Beware Of Dangerous Practices

Never ride against traffic. Failure to observe this rule causes the majority of car-bicycle collisions. Motorists can't always avoid the maneuvers of a wrong-way rider since the car and bike move toward each other very quickly.

Never make a left turn from the right lane.

Never pass through an intersection at full speed.

Never ignore stop light or stop signs.

Never enter traffic suddenly from a driveway or sidewalk. This rule is particularly important when the rider is a child, who is more difficult for a motorist to see.

Don't wear headphones that make it hard to hear and quickly respond to traffic.

Don't carry passengers on a bike. The only exception is a child under 40 lbs. who is buckled into an approved bike safety seat and wears a helmet as required by law.

Passenger trailers can be safe and fun. Be aware, though, that a trailer makes the bike much longer and requires careful control. Passengers must wear helmets.

What To Look For In A Bicycle Helmet

We endorse these guidelines for bicycle helmets recommended by the American Academy of Pediatrics:

The helmet should meet the voluntary testing standards of one of these two groups: American National Standards Institute (ANSI) OR Snell Memorial Foundation. Look for a sticker on the inside of the helmet.

1.) Select the right size. Find one that fits comfortably and doesn't pinch.
2.) Buy a helmet with a durable outer shell and a polystyrene liner. Be sure it allows adequate ventilation.
3.) Use the adjustable foam pads to ensure a proper fit at the front, back and sides.
4.) Adjust the strap for a snug fit. The helmet should cover the top of your forehead and not rock side to side or back and forth with the chain strap in place.
5.) Replace your helmet if it is involved in an accident.

Emergency Toolkit

When venturing out on bicycle tours, it is always smart to take along equipment to help make roadside adjustments and repairs. It is not necessary for every member of your group to carry a complete set of equipment, but make sure someone in your group brings along the equipment listed below:

1.) Standard or slotted screwdriver
2.) Phillips screwdriver
3.) 6" or 8" adjustable wrench
4.) Small pliers
5.) Spoke adjuster
6.) Tire pressure gauge
7.) Portable tire pump
8.) Spare innertube
9.) Tire-changing lugs

A Few Other Things

When embarking on a extended bike ride, it is important to give your bike a pre-ride check. To ensure that your bike is in premium condition, go over the bike's mechanisms, checking for any mechanical problems. It's best to catch these at home, and not when they occur "on the road." If you run into a problem that you can't fix yourself, you should check your local yellow pages for a professional bike mechanic.

When you are planning a longer trip, be sure to consider your own abilities and limitations, as well as those of any companions who may be riding with you. In general, you can ride about three times the length (time-wise) as your average training ride. If you have a regular cycling routine, this is a good basis by which to figure the maximum distance you can handle.

Finally, be aware of the weather. Bring plenty of sunblock for clear days, and rain gear for the rainy one. Rain can make some rides miserable, in addition to making it difficult to hear other traffic. Winds can blow up sand, and greatly increase the difficulty of a trail.

Trail Courtesy & Common Sense

1.) Stay on designated trails.
2.) Bicyclists use the right side of the trail (Walkers use the left side of the trail).
3.) Bicyclists should only pass slower users on the left side of the trail; use your voice to warn others when you need to pass.
4.) Get off to the side of the trail if you need to stop.
5.) Bicyclists should yield to all other users.
6.) Do not use alcohol or drugs while on the trail.
7.) Do not litter.
8.) Do not trespass onto adjacent land.
9.) Do not wear headphones while using the trail.

Health Hazards

Hypothermia

Hypothermia is a condition where the core body temperature falls below 90 degrees. This may cause death.

Mild hypothermia
1. Symptoms
   a. Pronounced shivering
   b. Loss of physical coordination
   c. Thinking becomes cloudy

2. Causes
   a. Cold, wet, loss of body heat, wind

3. Treatment
   a. Prevent further heat loss, get out of wet clothing and out of wind. Replace wet clothing with dry.
   b. Help body generate more heat. Refuel with high-energy foods and a hot drink, get moving around, light exercise, or external heat.

Severe hypothermia
1. Symptoms
   a. Shivering stops, pulse and respiration slows down, speech becomes incoherent.

2. Treatment
   a. Get help immediately.
   b. Don't give food or water.
   c. Don't try to rewarm the victim in the field.
   d. A buildup of toxic wastes and tactic acid accumulates in the blood in the body's extremities. Movement or rough handling will cause a flow of the blood from the extremities to the heart. This polluted blood can send the heart into ventricular fibrillations (heart attack). This may result in death.
   e. Wrap victim in several sleeping bags and insulate from the ground.

Frostbite

Symptoms of frostbite may include red skin with white blotches due to lack of circulation. Rewarm body part gently. Do not immerse in hot water or rub to restore circulation, as both will destroy skin cell.

Health Hazards (continued)

Heat Exhaustion

Cool, pale, and moist skin, heavy sweating, headache, nausea, dizziness and vomiting. Body temperature nearly normal.

Treatment: Have victim lie in the coolest place available – on back with feet raised. Rub body gently with cool, wet cloth. Give person glass of water every 15 minutes if conscious and can tolerate it. Call for emergency medical assistance.

Heat Stroke

Hot, red skin, shock or unconsciousness; high body temperature.

Treatment: Treat as a life-threatening emergency. Call for emergency medical assistance immediately. Cool victim by any means possible. Cool bath, pour cool water over body, or wrap wet sheets around body. Give nothing by mouth.

Explanation of Geological Terms

Bog
An acidic wetland that is fed by rainwater and is characterized by open water with a floating mat of vegetation (e.g. sedges, mosses, tamarack) that will often bounce if you jump on it.

Bluff
A high steep bank with a broad, flat, or rounded front.

Canyon
A deep, narrow valley with precipitous sides, often with a stream flowing through it.

Fen
An alkaline wetland that is fed by ground water and is often seen as a wet meadow and characterized by plants like grass or parnasis and sedges that grow in alkaline water.

Forest
A vegetative community dominated by trees and many containing understory layers of smaller trees, shorter shrubs and an herbaceous layers at the ground.

Grove
A small wooded area without underbrush, such as a picnic area.

Herb
A seed producing annual, biennial, or perennial that does not develop persistent woody tissue but dies down at the end of a growing season.

Karst
An irregular limestone region with sinks, underground streams, and caverns.

Lake
A considerable inland body of standing water.

Marsh
A wetland fed by streams and with shallow or deep water. Often characterized by mats of cattail, bulrushes, sedges and wetland forbs.

Mesic
A type of plant that requires a moderate amount of water.

Moraine
Long, irregular hills of glacial till deposited by stagnant and etreating glaciers.

Natural Community
A group of living organisms that live in the same place, e.g. woodland or prairie.

Explanation of Geological Terms (continued)

Park — An area maintained in its natural state as a public property.

Pond — A body of water usually smaller than a lake.

Prairie — Primarily treeless grassland community characterized by full sun and dominated by perennial, native grasses and forbs. Isolated remnants of tall grass prairie can be found along and near the I&M Corridor.

Preserve — An area restricted for the protection and preservation of natural resources.

Ridge — A range of hills or mountains.

Savanna — A grassland ecosystem with scattered trees characterized by native grasses and forbs.

Sedges — Grass-like plants with triangular stems and without showy flowers. Many are dominant in sedge meadows, bogs and fens but others are found in woodlands or prairies.

Shrubs — Low woody plants, usually shorter than trees and with several stems.

Swale — A lower lying or depressed and off wet stretch of land.

Swamp — Spongy land saturated and sometimes partially or intermittently covered with water.

Turf — The upper stratum of soil bound by grass and plant roots into a thick mat.

Wetland — The low lying wet area between higher ridges.

Riding Tips

- Pushing in gears that are too high can push knees beyond their limits. Avoid extremes by pedaling faster rather than shifting into a higher gear.

- Keeping your elbows bent, changing your hand position frequently and wearing bicycle gloves all help to reduce the numbness or pain in the palm of the hand from long-distance riding.

- Keep you pedal rpms up on an uphill so you have reserve power if you lose speed.

- Stay in a high-gear on a level surface, placing pressure on the pedals and resting on the handle bars and saddle.

- Lower your center of gravity on a long or steep downhill run by using the quick release seat post binder and dropping the saddle height down.

- Brake intermittently on a rough surface.

- Wear proper equipment. Wear a helmet that is approved by the Snell Memorial Foundation or the American National Standards Institute. Look for one of their stickers inside the helmet.

- Use a lower tire inflation pressure for riding on unpaved surfaces. The lower pressure will provide better tire traction and a more comfortable ride.

- Apply your brakes gradually to maintain control on loose gravel or soil.

- Ride only on trails designated for bicycles or in areas where you have the permission of the landowner.

- Be courteous to hikers or horseback riders on the trail, they have the right of way.

- Leave riding trails in the condition you found them. Be sensitive to the environment. Properly dispose of your trash. If you open a gate, close it behind you.

- Don't carry items or attach anything to your bicycle that might hinder your vision or control.

- Don't wear anything that restricts your hearing.

- Don't carry extra clothing where it can hang down and jam in a wheel.

Explanation of Symbols

TRAIL LEGEND

———————	Multi-Use Bike Trail
≈≈≈≈≈≈≈≈≈	Proposed Trail
⋕ ⋕ ⋕ ⋕	Alternate Trail
•••••••••◄	Hiking Trail
⋕⋕⋕⋕⋕⋕⋕	Equestrian Trail
———————	Paved Road
– – – – – –	Unpaved Road
———————	Road/Highway
+++++++++++	Railroad Tracks
–•–•–•–•–	Power/Pipe Line
– – – – – –	Boundary Line

TRAIL USE LEGEND

	Leisure Biking
	Mountain Biking
	Hiking
	Cross-country Skiing
	Horseback Riding
	Rollerblading
	Other

SYMBOL LEGEND

🏖	Beach/Swimming
🚲	Bicycle Repair
🏚	Cabin
Ⓐ	Camping
🛶	Canoe Launch
🛶	Canoeing
✚	First Aid
🅜	Food
GC	Golf Course
?	Information
🛏	Lodging
MF	Multi-Facilities
P	Parking
🛆	Picnic
🏛	Ranger Station
🚹🚺	Restrooms
🏠	Shelter
T	Trailhead/Access
🏛	Visitor/Nature Center
⛲	Water
🔭	Overlook/Observation

AREA LEGEND

▨	City, Town
▨	Parks, Preserves
▨	Waterway
●	Marsh/Wetland
★	Points of Interest
🌲	Forest/Woods

Bicycle Components & Tips

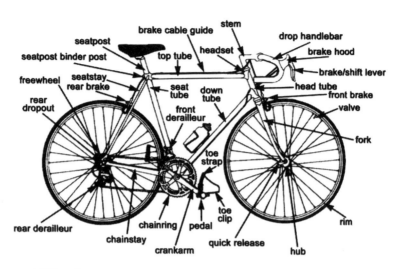

Tires and Wheels

Inspect your tire's thread for embedded objects, such a glass, and re-move to avoid potential punctures. Carry with you a spare tube, a patch kit, tire levers for removing the tire, and some duct tape. Don't reassemble the wheel when fixing a flat until you have felt around the inside the tire. The cause of the puncture could still be lodged there. Adjust your tire inflation pressure based on the type of ride. Lower pressure is better for off road biking or riding in the rain. A higher tire pressure is best for normal road biking or racing. Sometimes a clicking sound is caused by two spokes rubbing together. Try a little oil on the spokes where they cross.

Reflectors

Have at least a rear reflector on your bike. Reflectors on the back of your pedals is an effective way of alerting motorists' to your presence.

Pedals

A few drops of oil to the cleat where it contacts the pedal will help silence those clicks and creaks in clipless pedals.

Saddles

Replace an uncomfortable saddle with one that contains gel or extra-dense foam. Select a saddle best designed for your anatomy. Women generally have a wider distance than men between their bones that con-tact the saddle top.

Chains and Derailleurs

Avoid combining the largest rear cog with the large chainring or the small-est cog with the small chainring. Noises from the crank area may mean the chain is rubbing the front derailleur. To quiet this noise, move the front derailleur lever enough to center the chain through the cage but not cause a shift.

Massachusetts State Outline

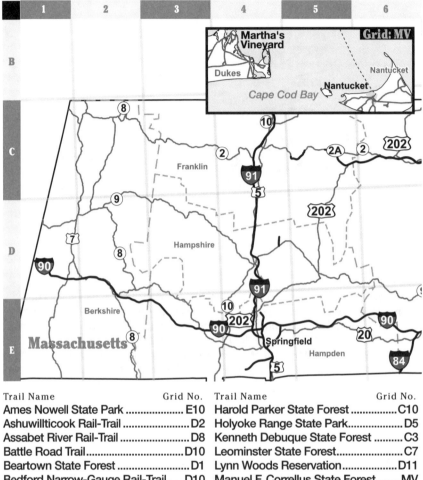

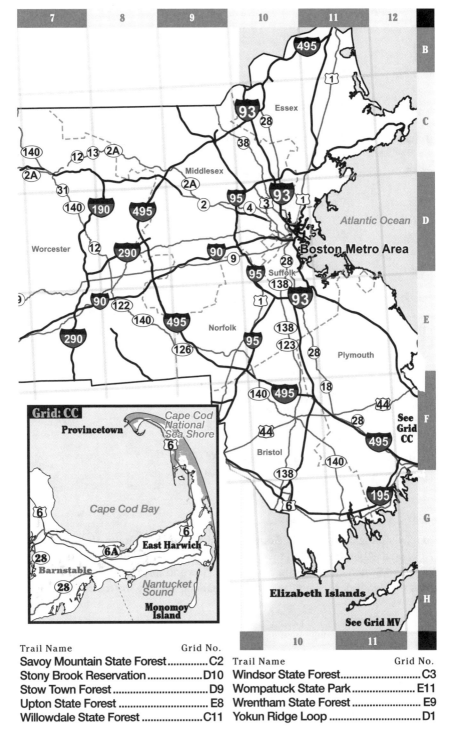

Ames Nowell State Park

Grid	E10
Length	12 miles
Surface	Singletrack, doubletrack
Setting	Cleveland pond, woods
Difficulty	Easy to moderate
Acres	607
Hours	Summer hours are dawn to dusk
Vicinity	Brockton, Abington
Lat/Long	42-07/70-59 Entrance off Linwood Street
County	Plymouth
Contact	Ames Nowell State Park Linwood Street, Abington 781-857-1336
Facilities	P ⟨M⟩ ⟨⟩

Getting There

From Boston take Route 3 to Route 18 (Exit 16), then on Route 18 to Route 123 West at Abington. Head toward Brockton for a mile, then turn right onto Groveland Street. Take another right onto Linwood Street to the stone gates at the park entrance. Past the gates is a parking area by the restrooms.

Trail Notes

Ames Nowell State Park is located south of Boston in southeast Massachusetts. This is a year-round use area with recreational activity centered around Cleveland Pond. Facilities here include a large parking and picnic area. Your ride will provide a view of the pond more often than not. Trail maintenance and expansion has been improving over the past several years. The trails are closed to motorized vehicles. Generally, the terrain consists of smooth singletrack, but expect occasional sections of rocks and roots. Some of the trails had been created some time ago by ATV's and off-road motorcycles, although the park does not allow motorized vehicles. NEMBA volunteers have been active in upgrading and maintaining the park's trails over the past few years. Remember that Ames Nowell is popular with hunters during hunting season.

Biking is allowed on the all the park's trails and roads, except for the trail that follows the eastern shoreline of Cleveland Pond. Getting lost should not be a problem as the park is bounded on all sides by paved road, and intersected by two power lines. You can access the park before the gates are open or after they close by parking outside the gates.

One of the easier trails is the path on high ground running from the ball field to the northern end of Cleveland Pond. The trail on the eastern shoreline of the pond is one of the more difficult. On the other side of the pond is a fairly easy trail leading to a boardwalk and then to another trail that takes you to a peninsula that juts out into the center of the pond. You can make a continuous loop of the park by combining some of the hiking trails, access roads, paved roads, and power line routes. Take the old fire roads at the western end of the dam out past the power line to get to the trails taking you into the back of the park. In the western most area of the park are many large boulders, some of which the trail leads you over the top rather than around.

TRAIL LEGEND	
••••••••••	Hiking Trail
————	Paved Road
– – – – – –	Unpaved Road
━━━━━	Road/Highway
⊹⊹⊹⊹⊹⊹	Power Line
– – – – –	Boundary Line

Ames Nowell State Park (continued)

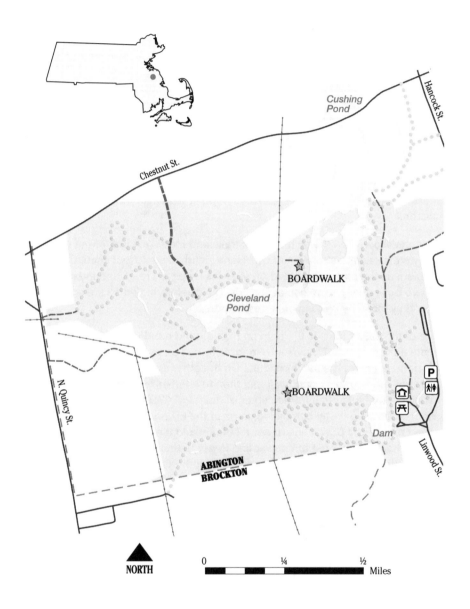

Ashuwillticook Rail Trail

Grid	D2
Length	11 miles
Surface	Asphalt
Setting	Rural, wetlands, lake and river fronts
Difficulty	Easy
Hours	Dawn to dusk
Vicinity	Lanesborough, Cheshire, Adams
Lat/Long	42-29/73-12 Hwy 8 & Berkshire Mall Road
County	Bristol
Contact	Ashuwillticook Rail Trail
	Dept of Conservation & Recreation
	Western Regional Headquarters
	413-442-8928
Facilities	

Getting There

Ashuwillitocook Rail Trail is located in the central-northern Berkshires in western Massachusetts.

From the South: Take I-90 to Route 20 (Exit 2) in Lee. Follow Route 20 west to Route 7 north for 11 miles to downtown Pittsfield. At the Park Square rotary follow East Street for 3.3 miles to the intersection of Route 9 and Route 8. Continue straight through the intersection for 1.5 miles to Berkshire Mall Road. Turn left for the entrance and parking.

From the North: Take Route 2 in downtown North Adams to Route 8 south for 5.5 miles to Adams center. Look for the brown Ashuwillticook signs. Turn left onto Hoosac Street, and then right onto Depot Street. There is parking

Ashuwillticook Rail Trail (continued)

at the Berkshires Visitor Center on the left. The trail is behind the Visitors Center. Additional parking is available at Farnams Road and Church Street in Cheshire, and in Adams at Russell Field off Harmony Street.

Trail Notes

This 10 foot wide rail trail runs parallel to Route 8 through the towns of Cheshire, Lanesborough, and Adams. The southern end of the trail begins at the entrance to the Berkshire Mall off Route 8 in Lanesborough and travels north to the center of Adams with its restored main street. Parking and restrooms are available at several locations along the way. The trail follows the railroad corridor of the Pittsfield & North Adams Railroad as you proceed north from Lanesborouth. You will pass forested areas, lakes, and ponds. About a quarter of your way into the ride, you'll come to Cheshire Reservoir where bird watching and fishing are popular. It passes through the Hoosic River Valley, between the Mount Greylock and the Hoosac Mountain Ranges. The "Discover the Berkshires Visitor Center", located at the northern trailhead in Adams, offers visitor information, lodging reservations, restrooms, and exhibits and is open from 8:30 am to 5 pm. Comfort stations are located at the trail parking area off Berkshire Mall Road and Farnams Road, and are open between mid-May to mid-September during daylight hours. As an option in case you prefer public transportation for your return trip, you can catch Berkshire Regional Transit Authority bus back to the Berkshire Mall. The buses can accommodate bikes, but are generally limited to two.

The name Ashuwillticook derives from the Native American word phrase meaning "the pleasant river in between the hills". The Pittsfield & North Adams Railroad first developed the rail corridor in 1845. It was taken over by the Boston and Maine Railroad in 1981 until rail service was abandoned in 1990.

TRAIL LEGEND	
————	Multi-Use Bike Trail
– – – – –	Appalachian Trail
————	Road/Highway
+++++++++	Railroad Tracks

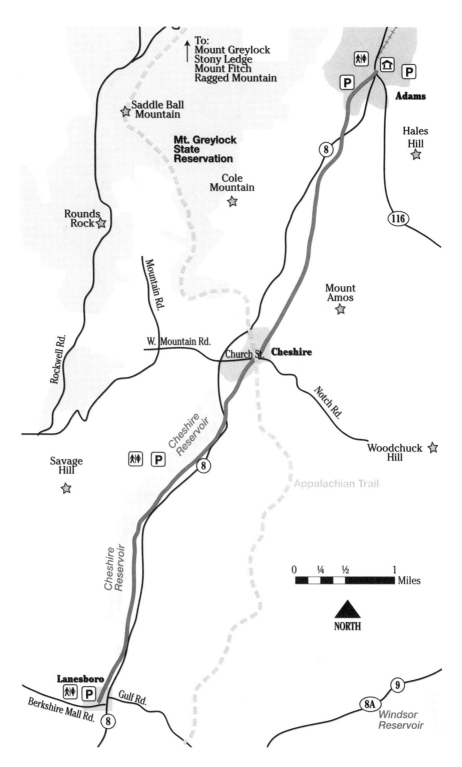

To:
Mount Greylock
Stony Ledge
Mount Fitch
Ragged Mountain

Adams

Hales
Hill ☆

Saddle Ball
Mountain ☆

**Mt. Greylock
State
Reservation**

8

116

Cole
Mountain
☆

Rounds
Rock ☆

Mountain Rd.

Mount
Amos
☆

Rockwell Rd.

W. Mountain Rd.

Church St. **Cheshire**

Notch Rd.

Cheshire
Reservoir

Appalachian Trail

Woodchuck ☆
Hill

Savage
Hill
☆

8

0   ¼   ½   1
▮▮▮▮▮▮▮▮ Miles

Cheshire
Reservoir

▲
NORTH

Lanesboro

9

Gulf Rd.

8A

Berkshire Mall Rd.

8

*Windsor
Reservoir*

Assabet River Rail Trail

Grid	D8
Length	5.5 miles, 12.5 total miles slated
Surface	Paved, 12 feet wide
Setting	Suburban, scenic overlooks
Difficulty	Easy
Vicinity	Hudson, Marlborough
Lat/Long	42-23/71-34 Town of Hudson
County	Middlesex
Contact	ARRT Municipal Coordinator Town Hall, 78 Main Street Hudson, MA 01749 978-562-9963
Facilities	

Getting There

To Hudson: From I-495, east on Route 117 to get to Maynard, then east on Route 62 to get to Hudson. Continue into town and through the rotary to Wilkins Street and a parking Lot.

To Marlborough: From I-495, take US 20/Granger Boulevard east to get to Marlborough. Take a left on Route 85/Bolton Street, then left on Union Street, and left again on Hudson Street.

Parking areas include trailhead off Wilkins Street in Hudson and off Hudson Street across from Kelleher Field and Jefferson Street in Marlborough.

Trail Notes

The trail begins along Route 62 in Hudson or at Lincoln Street and Highland Street in Marlborough. At the Hudson trailhead is a restored blue caboose and an ice cream store across the road. The caboose is open to the public. As you pass through Hudson, you'll have to leave the trail to get through a three-way intersection at Broad Street, Villa de Porto Boulevard, and the South Street extension. Back on the trail you cross a wooden bridge, along forest, and through a tunnel. It passes the Boston Scientific medical center to an intersection at Fitchburg Street. Following the intersection and some heavy traffic you'll come to spurs connecting you to Assebet River. From Hudson the trail will eventually link Stow, Maynard and Acton. Phase 1 of the slated 12.5-miles opened in September of 2006.

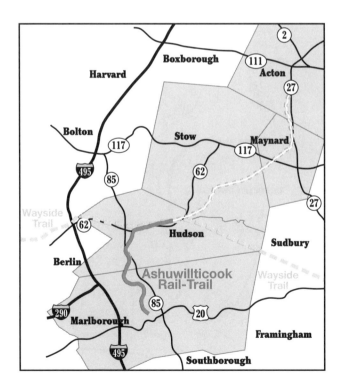

Assabet River Rail Trail (continued)

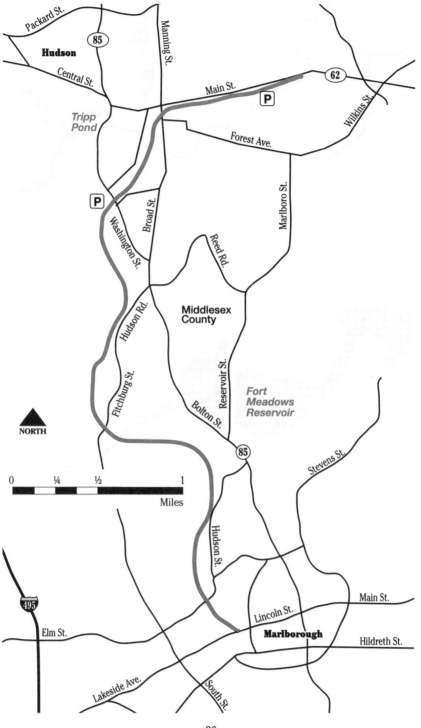

Beartown State Forest

Grid	D1
Length	12 miles
Surface	Forest trails, roads
Setting	Forest, large pond
Difficulty	Moderate
Acres	12,000
Fees	$5 per vehicle – May through mid-October
Hours	8 am to 8 pm
Vicinity	Monterey, Great Barrington
Lat/Long	42-12/73-17 Livermore Peak
County	Berkshire
Contact	Beartown State Forest 69 Blue Hill Road Monterey, MA 91245 413-528-0904
Facilities	P ♦♦ 🌲 🍴 🏕 🏊

Getting There

From the East or West - Take Exit 2 in Lee, and follow Route 102 west for 4.7-miles to Stockbridge. Turn left and follow Route 7 south for 6-miles to Great Barrington, then turn left on Route 23 east for 5.3-miles to Monterey. Turn left on Blue Hill Road for 2.2-miles to the park entrance (Benedict Pond Road) on the right.

From the North or South – From Route 7 in Great Barrington, take Route 23 east for 5.3 miles to Monterey. From there turn left onto Blue Hill Road for 2.2-miles to the part entrance on the right.

Beartown State Forest (continued)

Trail Notes

Beartown State Forest, located in the heart of the Berkshires, offers an extensive network of trails over its 12,000 acres, providing a chance to observe deer, bobcat, and even its namesake, the Black Bear. The summer months advertise its deciduous forest, with flowering shrubs and wildflowers. Summertime is also an opportunity to enjoy a swim at the pristine 35-acre Benedict Pond. The famous Appalachian Trail also runs through the forest for about 7.5 miles. It can be accessed from a parking area near the intersection of Routes 23 & 57, at Great Barrington-Monterey town line, and on Main Road in Tyringham. Cultural attractions include the Tanglewood Music Festival and Jacob's Pillow Dance Theater.

The initial phase of your ride takes you for a climb for a mile or so on rugged double-track, with loose rock and washouts on the steeper sections. From there, you're on single-track trails for several miles before descending to dirt roads. You will be surprised at the beauty and mountainous of this area. The miles of trails go far back into fantastic hardwood forest. The more north you go, the more remote it is. Closer to the parking lot are more moderate rides with scenic views. There are some nice overlooks on mountain spots little more than a mile in from the main parking lot. The beach area can get busy with visitors, especially on weekends, although the far side away from the main beach tends to be more serene and peaceful. The ranger's station is a couple miles southeast of the main parking lot and the beach/campground area. Forest facilities include campsites with showers and picnic areas. Most all services can be found in Stockbridge and Lee to the north, and Great Barrington to the west.

TRAIL LEGEND	
────────	Multi-Use Bike Trail
─ ─ ─ ─ ─	Appalachian Trail
••••••••••	Hiking Trail
▥▥▥▥▥▥▥▥	Equestrian/MB Trail
────────	Paved Road
─ ─ ─ ─ ─	Unpaved Road
────────	Road/Highway
•─•─•─•─•	Power Line
─ ─ ─ ─ ─	Boundary Line

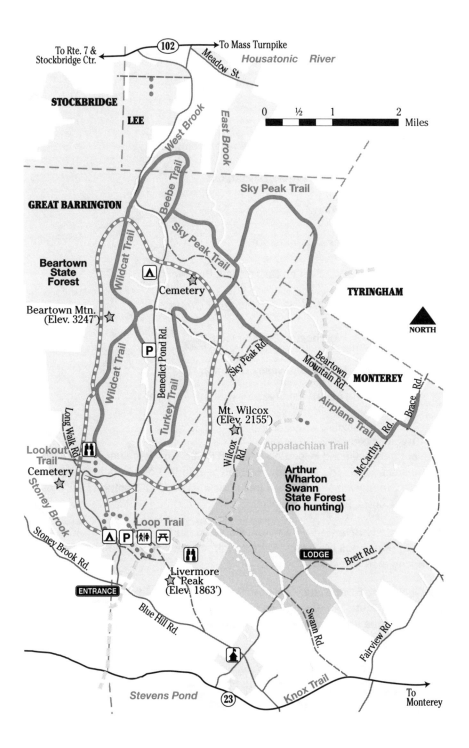

To Rte. 7 &
Stockbridge Ctr.

102

To Mass Turnpike

Housatonic River

Meadow St.

STOCKBRIDGE

LEE

West Brook

East Brook

0   ½   1   2   Miles

GREAT BARRINGTON

Beebe Trail

Sky Peak Trail

Wildcat Trail

Sky Peak Trail

Beartown
State
Forest

Cemetery

Beartown Mtn.
(Elev. 3247')

TYRINGHAM

NORTH

Benedict Pond Rd.

Sky Peak Rd.

Beartown
Mountain Rd

MONTEREY

Wildcat Trail

Turkey Trail

Airplane Trail

McCarthy Rd.

Brace Rd.

Mt. Wilcox
(Elev. 2155')

Appalachian Trail

Long Walk Rd.

Lookout
Trail
Cemetery

Wilcox Rd.

Arthur
Wharton
Swann
State Forest
(no hunting)

Stoney Brook

Loop Trail

Stoney Brook Rd.

LODGE

Brett Rd.

ENTRANCE

Livermore
Peak
(Elev. 1863')

Blue Hill Rd.

Swann Rd.

Fairview Rd.

Stevens Pond

23

Knox Trail

To
Monterey

Blackstone River Bikeway

Grid	E8-10
Length	12.5 miles, 48-miles when complete
Surface	Paved, gravel, ballast, dirt
Setting	Urban
Difficulty	Easy to moderate
Vicinity	Worchester, Blackstone, Providence RI
Lat/Long	42-17/71-47 Plummer Corner
County	Worchester, Providence RI
Contact	Blackstone Valley Chamber of Commerce 508-234-9090
Facilities	

Getting There

The northern trailhead is located at Union Station in Worcester, off I-290 and by the rail tracks. The southern trailhead is at India Point Park in East Providence. Currently, the completed trail ends at Valley Fall Heritage Park by Mill Street in Central Falls, Rhode Island.

To Blackstone River State Park from Route 95 North: Take Route 146 (Exit 23) north to Breakneck Hill Road/Route 123 (becomes Front Street) eastbound to a parking area located on the left.

To Blackstone River State Park from Route 95 South: Take Route 295 (Exit 4) south to Route 146 (Exit 9A) and then south to Breakneck Hill Road/Route 123. Continue eastbound on Breakneck Hill Road, which becomes Front Street, to a parking area on the left.

To get to the Route 116 (George Washington Highway) parking area in Lincoln, take Route 295 north to Mendon Road (Exit 10), then left to its intersection with Route 116/George Washington Hwy. Take a right (eastbound) for about a mile to the parking area on the right.

Trail Notes

There are currently 12.5 miles completed of this eventual 48-mile trail system. The completed sections include ten miles in Rhode Island and 2.5 miles in Massachusetts. The route passes through historic Blackstone River Valley, and connects Providence, Rhode Island with Worcester, Massachusetts. The 2.5-mile section in Massachusetts was opened in 2005. When completed it will extend from the City Common in Worcester to the Rhode Island state line. As the planned bikeway winds south from downtown Worcester, it will pass through several historic mill villages and state/local parks. Highlights include Blackstone River and Canal Heritage State Park, where remnants of the Blackstone Canal still remain. The interim route consists mostly of local roadways.

Rhode Island has completed 10-miles of this off-road bikeway, extending from Valley Falls Heritage Park on the Cumberland/Central Fall line north to the Woonsocket city line. The largest trailhead is off Front Street in Lincoln, but there are numerous trailhead parking areas along the way. Interim on-road routes stretch south to Providence. From India Point Park in Providence you can connect to the 14.5 mile East Bay Bikepath. This trail travels along Narragansett Bay to the waterfront community of Bristol, Rhode Island.

The DCR's Division of State Parks and Recreation

This Division is responsible for the maintenance and management of over 430,000 acres of privately and state-owned forest and parks, nearly 10% of the Commonwealth's total land mass. Within the lands managed by the Division of State Parks and Recreation are some 29 campgrounds, over 2,000 miles of trails, 87 beaches, 37 swimming, wading, and spray pools, 62 camp-grounds, 55 ballfields, and 145 miles of paved bike and rail trails.

Massachusetts Segment

NORTH

Worcester

Auburn

Dorothy Pond

Martin St.

Granite St.

Millbury

Singletary Pond

Grafton St.

Grafton

Sutton

Boston Rd.

Central Turnpike

Saundersville

Fisherville

Maple Ave.

Sutton St.

Sutton State Forest

Hill St.

Whitins Pond

Whitinsville

Fowler Rd.

Northbridge

Riverdale

Fletcher St.

Church St.

Linwood

Blackstone River & Canal Heritage State Park

W. Hartford Ave.

Douglas St.

Uxbridge

Mendon Rd.

Snett

Blackstone St.

Massachusetts
Rhode Island

Millville

Blackstone

Snett

N. Smithfield

Rhode Island Segment

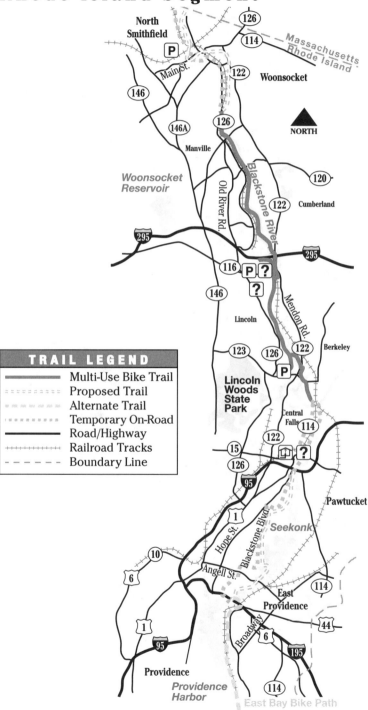

TRAIL LEGEND

————————	Multi-Use Bike Trail
- - - - - - - - -	Proposed Trail
— — — — —	Alternate Trail
· · · · · · · · · ·	Temporary On-Road
————————	Road/Highway
+++++++++	Railroad Tracks
– – – – –	Boundary Line

North Smithfield

126

114

Massachusetts Rhode Island

P

Main St.

122

Woonsocket

146

126

146A

Manville

NORTH

Woonsocket Reservoir

Old River Rd.

Blackstone River

120

122

Cumberland

295

295

116

P ?

146

?

Mendon Rd.

Lincoln

123

126

122

Berkeley

P

Lincoln Woods State Park

Central Falls

114

122

15

126

?

95

Pawtucket

1

Hope St.

Blackstone Blvd.

Seekonk

10

6

Angell St.

114

East Providence

1

6

44

95

195

Providence

Providence Harbor

114

East Bay Bike Path

The Blackstone River Bikeway

Courtesy of the Massachusetts Department of Conservation & Recreation. Photo by Paul Meleski for the DCR.

Bradley Palmer State Park

Grid	C11
Length	35 miles
Surface	Singletrack, doubletrack
Setting	Woods, rolling meadows
Difficulty	Easy to moderate
Acres	721
Fees	$5 per car to park by the wading pool
Hours	Sunrise to sunset
Vicinity	Ipswich, Asbury Grove
Lat/Long	42-39/70-54 Entrance off Bradley Palmer State Road
County	Essex
Contact	Bradley Palmer State Park Asbury Street in Topsfield 978-887-5931
Facilities	

Getting There

From Boston, take Route 128 North to Route 1A North (Exit 20A). Continue on Route 1A until Wenham. Turn left on Arbor Road (becomes Highland Street) and continue straight at the intersection with Asbury Grove. Continue for 1 mile to Bradley Palmer's unpaved parking area on the left, about 100 yards before a gate barring a side road.

From Newburyport take Route 1 south for about 8 miles to Topsfield. Turn left onto Ipswich Road for 1.2 miles to Asbury Street and then take a right. The park entrance is approximately ¼ miles on the left.

Trail Notes

Bradley Palmer State Park is located in northeastern Massachusetts. The trails vary from needled paths, to packed dirt, sandy fire roads, and rocky areas. The main road along the pool is closed to car traffic, making the park easy and safer to explore, especially with little ones along. Generally you will park on the small, unpaved lot about 200 yards before the entrance, as the parking lots inside the park are rarely open. You avoid the parking fees by parking at this entrance. The park's wading pool is large and shallow. It is open during the summer from 10 am to 4 pm. There is a $5.00 daily use fee. Bathrooms and lifeguards are provided, but food is not available. There is a drinking fountain by the pool that is only available during the open pool season.

The majority of your riding opportunities are on wide and level doubletrack paths that frequently intersect. The two hills, Blueberry and Moon, offer some nice singletrack downhills as they wind around the face of these short hills. The river trail is scenic and narrow, but you may find it muddy. The well traveled trails are marked and maintained. It is not too difficult to stay oriented with nearby landmarks such as paved park road, the Ipswich River, and open fields along the east side of the park.

The park was developed from the estate of businessman, lawyer, and benefactor Bradley Palmer. Construction of his mansion, located in back of park headquarters near the Nature Trail, began in 1902. Palmer, influenced by Boston's Arnold Arboretum, planted fruit trees, evergreens, and flowering shrubs from all over the United States, and elsewhere. In that Palmer had no heir, he willed his estate to the commonwealth of Massachusetts.

TRAIL LEGEND	
━━━━━━	Multi-Use Bike Trail
▬ ▬ ▬ ▬ ▬	Interpretive Trail
────────	Paved Road
·–·–·–·–·	Unpaved Road
━━━━━━	Road/Highway
– – – – – –	Boundary Line

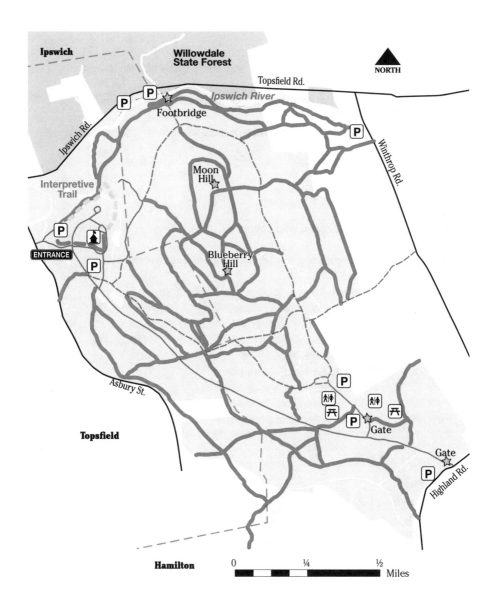

Ipswich

Willowdale
State Forest

NORTH

Topsfield Rd.

Ipswich River

Footbridge

Ipswich Rd.

Winthrop Rd.

Moon
Hill

Interpretive
Trail

ENTRANCE

Blueberry
Hill

Asbury St.

Topsfield

Gate

Gate

Highland Rd.

Hamilton

0   ¼   ½
                              Miles

Callahan State Park

Grid	D9
Length	7 miles of marked trails, and many miles of unmarked trail
Surface	Packed dirt singletrack & doubletrack
Setting	Woods, open fields, rocky areas
Difficulty	Moderate
Acres	820
Hours	Dawn to dusk, year round
Vicinity	Framingham
Lat/Long	41-19/71-28 Access off Millwood Street
County	Middlesex
Contact	Callahan State Park Millwood Street, Framingham 508-653-9641
Facilities	P

Getting There

From Boston take I-90 west to Route 9, then east toward Framingham to
Edgell Road. Take a left (south) to Belknap Road, then left to Millwood Street
to the entrance and into a dirt parking area across from the golf course. You
can also take Route 30 to Woodmere, then north to its end. From there, take
a right and then the first left onto Millwood Street and the parking area across
from the golf course.

Trail Notes

Callahan State Park is located in northwest Framingham, west of Boston in east-central Massachusetts. While most of the park riding is moderate, the trails on the north side of Edmands and can be quite difficult. In general the terrain consists of dirt paths through some 100 acres of open fields, and singletrack rocky and root-laden climbs and descents. The toughest is probably the climb up Juniper Trail. There is an earthen dam that winds left around the bottom of the park, with a gravel and dirt doubletrack path on the top. This path provides access to several easy riding trails through the southern part of the park, Rocky Road Trail and Moore Road. The small side trails can end up taking you all over, and really extend your ride time. The Bay Circuit Trail also passes through Callahan.

Control Your Bicycle

Ride responsibly. Maintain a safe speed at all times and exercise caution on blind curves and steep slopes.

Always Yield Trail

Hikers and horseback riders have the right of way. When approaching from the rear, slow down and announce your presence. Pass slowly and safely.

Ride Safely

Always wear a helmet and consider wearing eye protection. Carry a water bottle and a repair kit. Be familiar with your bicycle. Know your limits.

Plan Ahead

Familiarize yourself with a trail map.

TO RTE. 20

Backpacker Trail

ENTRANCE

Broad Meadow Rd.

P ?

Acorn Trail

Back-packer Trail

Springhill Farm (Private)

Ways-ide Inn Rd.

Nixon Rd.

Bear Paw Trail

Parmenter Rd.

Pine Tree Loop

Gibbs Mountain

Pioneer Trail

Edmands Rd.

Sudbury Valley Trustees Conservation Land

Grove St.

P ?

Marlborough

Southborough

Pine Hill Rd.

NORTH

Red Tail Trail

Wren Trail

East-Leigh Farm
Juniper Trail
Deer Run Trail

Fox Hunt Trail

The Mead-ows

Welch Reservation

Packard Trail

Packard Pond

Winch Rd.

Pipeline Trail

Lady Slipper Trail

Chick A Dee Trail

Birch Trail

Eagle Trail

ENTRANCE

P ?

Moore St.

Pine cone Trail

Coco Ridge Trail

Earthen Dam

Millwood St.

Aqueduct

Framingham

| 0 | ¼ | ½ | | 1 |
Miles

TRAIL LEGEND

- ▬▬▬▬ Hiking Trail Unpaved Rd.
- ‑ ‑ ‑ Bay Circuit Trail
- •••••••• Hiking Trail
- ——— Paved Road
- ‑‑‑‑‑‑ Unpaved Road
- ▬▬▬ Road/Highway
- ‑+‑+‑+ Power Line
- ‑ ‑ ‑ ‑ Boundary Line

Cape Cod Canal

Grid	CC
Length	16 miles
Surface	Concrete
Terrain	Paved service roads on both sides of the Canal
Difficulty	Easy to moderate
Hours	Open year round
Vicinity	Bourne
Lat/Long	41-45/70-35 Bourne Recreation Area
County	Barnstable
Contact	U.S. Army Corps of Engineers 508-759-4431 Cape Cod Region Chamber of Commerce 508-759-6000
Facilities	

Getting There
From Boston, I-93 south to Route 3, then continue south to the Sagamore Bridge. Continue on Highway 6 across the bridge. Take Exit 1 off Highway 6 to Route 6A. Take Route 6A to the Bourne Recreation Area on the right.

Trail Notes
The bikeway follows the Cape Cod Canal connecting the Bourne and Sagamore Bridges.

It consists of 8-miles of service roads on each side of the Cape Cod Canal. These roads are limited to bicycling, and other non-motorized use except for authorized canal vehicles. There are minimal grades, and is ideal for beginner to casual cyclists, especially families with younger children. The surface is smooth concrete, with a yellow line painted down the center designating two-way traffic.

The canal separates Cape Cod from the rest of Massachusetts, and is maintained by the Army Corps of Engineers. The Cape Cod Canal is the world's widest sea-level canal, having a bottom width with a minimum of 480 feet. Spanning the waterway are two large bridges, about three miles apart. The wind at the top of these 135-foot high structures suggests it might be better to walk your bike across to avoid falling off the high curb into traffic or plowing into the steel fence. It's a beautiful ride with some great scenery and a great place to watch large ships and pleasure boats going through the canal between Cape Cod Bay and Buzzards Bay.

Parking areas, park benches, comfort stations and picnic areas are provided at various access points along both sides of the Canal. Be sure to visit the Cape Cod Canal Visitor Center. Its facilities include a theater showing continuous DVD presentations on Canal History, and a variety of interactive exhibits. Admission is free, and it is open from May to October.

Canal Service Roads – North Side	7.0 miles
Railroad Bridge to Bourne Bridge	1.25 miles
Bourne Bridge to Herring Run	2.25 miles
Herring Run to Sagamore Bridge	1.00 miles
Sagamore Bridge to east end	2.50 miles

Canal Service Road – South Side4	6.5 miles
Railroad Bridge to Bourne Bridge	1.25 miles
Bourne Bridge to Sagamore Bridge	3.25 miles
Sagamore Bridge to east end	2.00 miles

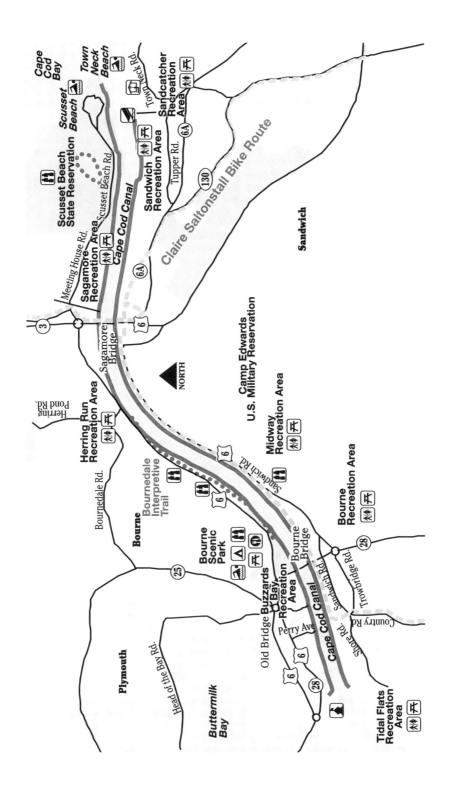

Cape Cod Rail-Trail

Grid	CC
Length	26 miles
Surface	Paved
Setting	Pine woods, salt marshes, ponds, easy hills
Difficulty	Easy
Vicinity	Wellfleet, Dennis
Lat/Long	41-42/70-06 Trailhead off Route 134
County	Barnstable, Howard
Contact	Nickerson State Park
	Massachusetts Dept of Conservation & Recreation
	251 Causeway Street, Ste 600
	Boston, MA 02114
	508-896-3491
Facilities	P ♦♦ ⊞ ⅍ ⵢ ▲ ⓪

Getting There

To get to the south trailhead in South Dennis, take Hwy 6 to Route 134 (Exit 9) and head south, past Cumberland Farms, for about a half-miles to trailhead parking on the left.

Trail parking:
- The western trailhead at Route 134 in South Dennis
- Headwater Drive in Harwich
- Route 137 in Brewster
- Nickerson State Park in Brewster
- Orleans Center
- Cap Cod National Seashore at the Salt Pond visitors Center in Eastham
- National Seashore at Marconi Area
- The eastern trailhead at LeCount Hollow Road in South Wellfleet

Trail Notes

The Cape Cod Rail Trail takes you on a former railroad right-of-way through the towns of Dennis, Harwich, Brewster, Orleans, Eastham and Wellfleet. The trail has well-marked automobile crossings and there are only a few hills. There is even a wide unpaved shoulder on one side for horseback riders, walkers, and joggers. Bike rentals are available at the bike shops in Eastham and Dennis, and at Nickerson State Park. Food, water, and restroom facilities are available at Nickerson State Park near the halfway point, Salt Pond visitors Center at Cape Cod National Seashore and the National Seashore Headquarters. Additional facilities at Nickerson State Park include camping, biking trails, swimming, boating, and fishing opportunities.

The western end of the trail takes you from Dennis into Brewster, winding through shaded woods, over easy hills, and past ponds with public beaches. The next leg takes you from Brewster to Salt Pond Road in Eastham, encompassing Nickerson State Park, with its beaches and campsites, and the galleries and shops in the town of Orleans. The eastern third of the trail goes from Eastham to Le Count Hollow road in Wellfleet. This section is straight and flat. A side trip might include a stop at the Cape Cod National Seashore Visitors Center to see its science and history exhibits. From the Visitors Center you can also take a ride through the oak woods and a marsh to Coast Guard Beach.

Cape Cod Rail-Trail (continued)

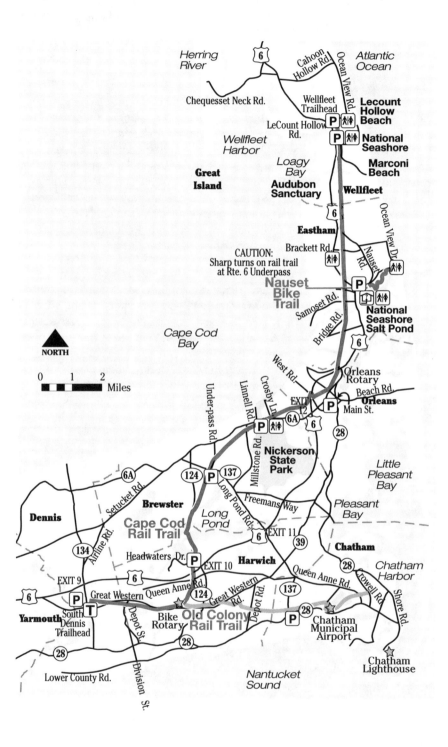

Charles River Bike Path
Dr. Paul Dudley White Bicycle Path

Grid	D10
Length	18 miles
Surface	Paved
Setting	Parkway, marshes, woods
Difficulty	Easy
Vicinity	Boston, Cambridge, Watertown
Lat/Long	42-02/71.04
County	Suffolk, Middlesex
Contact	Metropolitan District Commission 617-727-5114
Facilities	P 🚲 🏕

Getting There
From Boston take Storrow Drive west past the Harvard Square exit, then left onto Soldiers Field Road. Parking is available at the Metropolitan District Commission parking lots on Soldiers Field Road.

From the west take Route 2 toward Boston. Instead of bearing left when Route 2 heads for Cambridge and Memorial Drive, continue straight. Bear left where the road forks, through signal lights and a bridge, then a right onto Soldiers Field Road and a parking area.

Trail Notes
This 18-mile trail begins at Science Park, near the Museum of Science, the locks and dam, and runs along both sides of the Charles River to Watertown and back. You can enter and exit at many points in route. The trail is composed of two loops, the 11-mile Boston-Cambridge loop and the 7-mile Cambridge-Watertown loop. As a biker, you be sharing the path with joggers, walkers, vendors, and in-line skaters, so you will be competing for space on weekends and summer evenings.

Charles River Bike Path
Dr. Paul Dudley White Bicycle Path
(continued)

The Charles River Basin along the Boston side forms three discernible zones: the Lower Basin, from the historic Charles River Dam to the Boston University Bridge; the Middle Basin, from the Boston University Bridge to Herter Park, and the Upper Basin, from Herter Park to the Watertown Dam. The Lower Basin is 2.5 miles long and up to two thousand feet wide. It provides a panoramic image of Boston and Cambridge with sweeping views of the skyline, including the slope of Beacon Hill and the gold dome of the State House. The Middle Basin provides a transition from urban and formal to rural and natural. Parkways line the Basin separating it from contiguous open spaces. The largest open space is between the Harvard University athletic fields on the south and Mt. Auburn and Cambridge on the north. The Upper Charles is a more narrow body of water with small dams and arched bridges at intermittent intervals. Your views of the river ahead are short, extending on to the next bend in the river. The pathways border forested floodplains and shallow marshes, creating a self-sustaining natural environment. These areas support a wide diversity of bird, animal and plant life.

The Charles River Dam controls the water level in the river basin. An earlier dam built nearly a century ago and located beneath the Museum of Science, had the purpose of creating a fresh water basin and river front park in Boston. The newly landscaped banks of the river became known as the Charles River Esplanade. The later dam was completed in1978, and the Esplanade went through a major expansion, widening and lengthening the park land.

Available food and drink directly on the route is from vendors located adjacent to the Esplanade on the Boston side or near the road when Memorial Drive is closed to traffic on Sundays. Restrooms are available at the MDC Daly Recreation Center on Nonantum Street, the MDC boathouse between the Esplanade and the dam, by the Hatch Shell on the Esplanade, and at the Galleria mall.

Dr. Paul Dudley White was a pioneering cardiologist, and a founding member of the American Heart Association. He was born in Roxbury, Massachusetts and graduated from Harvard Medical School in 1911. He consulted on President Dwight D. Eisenhower when he suffered a heart attack during his second term in office. The Postal Service honored him with a 3-cent postage stamp in 1986. Dr. White emphasized fitness and exercise as one of the best ways to prevent cardiac disease, and was an avid cyclist.

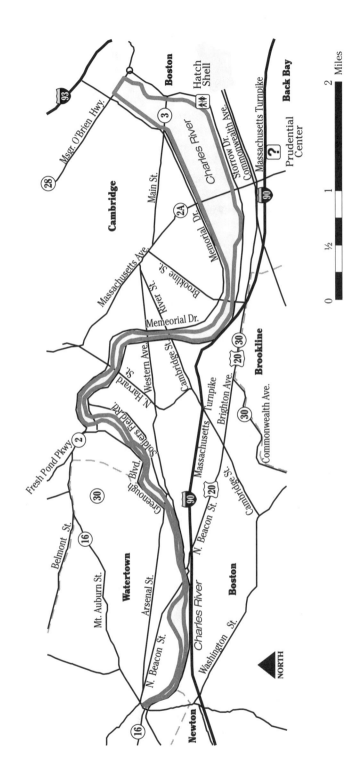

49

Cutler Park

Grid	E10
Length	10 miles
Surface	Singletrack, dirt roads
Setting	Woods, Cutler Pond, marsh
Difficulty	Easy to moderate
Acres	800
Hours	Dawn to dusk
Vicinity	Needham
Lat/Long	42-18/72-13 Cutler Park
County	Norfolk
Contact	Dept. of Conservation & Recreation Cutler Park 617-333-7405
Facilities	P

Getting There
From Highway 95, take Route 128 (Exit 95) in Needham heading east. Turn right on 2nd Avenue into an industrial park. Take a right on 4th Avenue, and then right again on Kendrick Street. The Cutler Park parking lot is about .2 miles further ahead on your left.

Trail Notes
Cutler Park comprises the largest remaining fresh water marsh on the middle Charles River. The marshlands are created by flooding from the Newton Upper Fall Silk Dam, and have been used for pasturelands for many years. In addition to Needham, the park extends into Dedham, Newton, Brookline and Boston. The more challenging singletrack are located between Kendrick Pond and Route 128. The singletracks nearest the highway provide some

roller coaster climbs and descents. To add to your exploring opportunities, there are many more trails not shown on the map that extend into the marshes on plank bridges.

The trail goes around Kendrick Pond and extends from the pond area to Powell's Island canoe landing, doubles back and goes under the MBTA commuter rail and out to the Great Plain. From there a left turn takes down a wide path alongside the elevated railroad line to the Charles River, directly across from Millennium Park. To extend your ride you can head into Riverdale Park, Millennium Park, the Brook Farm Conservation Area, and Newton's Nahanton Park for a loop of almost 16 miles. Cutler Park trails are closed to mountain biking from January 1 to April 15.

DCR Visitor Guidelines
The park is open dawn to dusk
Dogs must be leashed and waste removed
Mountain biking allowed on established trails from April 15 to December 31
Visitors must abide by park signage

The following is prohibited
Motorized vehicles
Hunting or trapping
Fires
Alcoholic beverages
Removal of any park resource
Failure to comply may result in arrest and/or fine per order of MGLC 92, S.37

Important Contacts
Emergency	911
24 Hour DCR Radio Dispatch	617-722-1188
State Police	508-820-2250

Cutler Park (continued)

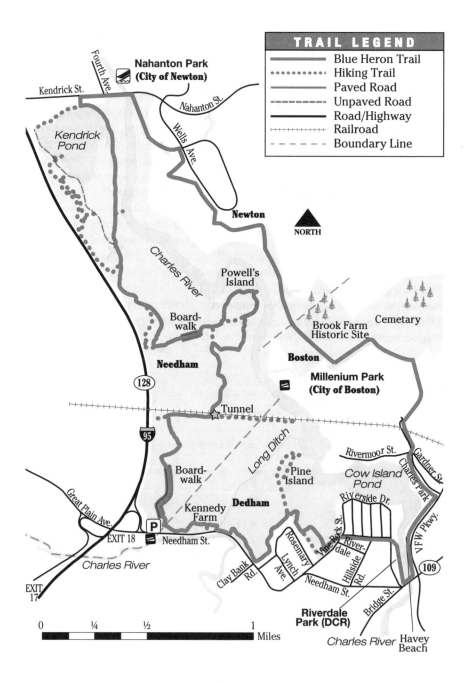

TRAIL LEGEND

————	Blue Heron Trail
••••••••••	Hiking Trail
————	Paved Road
- - - - -	Unpaved Road
▬▬▬▬	Road/Highway
+++++++	Railroad
– – – – –	Boundary Line

Fourth Ave.

Nahanton Park (City of Newton)

Kendrick St.

Nahanton St.

Kendrick Pond

Wells Ave.

Charles River

Newton

▲ NORTH

Powell's Island

Board-walk

Brook Farm Historic Site

Cemetary

Needham

Boston

128

Millenium Park (City of Boston)

95

Tunnel

Long Ditch

Rivermoor St.

Gardner St.

Charles Park

Board-walk

Pine Island

Cow Island Pond

Riverside Dr.

Great Plain Ave.

Dedham

Kennedy Farm

Vine Rock St.

River-dale

Hillside Rd.

VFW Pkwy.

P

EXIT 18

Needham St.

Rosemary Rd.

Lynch Ave.

Clay Bank Rd.

Needham St.

Bridge St.

109

Charles River

EXIT 17

Riverdale Park (DCR)

Charles River Havey Beach

0	¼	½	1

Miles

DAR State Forest

Grid	D3
Length	15 miles
Surface	Singletrack, dirt roads
Setting	Woods, Berkshire Mountain foothills
Difficulty	Easy to moderate, some difficult
Acres	1,770
Fees	$5 per vehicle from Memorial Day through mid-September
Hours	Sunrise to sunset
Vicinity	Goshen
Lat/Long	42-27/72-48 Parking area off Moore Hill
County	Hampshire
Contact	DAR State Forest 555 East Street Williamsburg, MA 61096 413-268-7098
Facilities	

Getting There

From the north via I-91 – take Route 2 (Exit 26) in Greenfield and head west for 9.8 miles to Route 112 south. Follow Route 112 south for 13 miles to the park entrance on the left.

From the south via I-91 – take Route 9 (Exit 19) in Northampton and proceed west for 15 miles to Goshen. Turn right on Route 112 north and continue for 0.7 miles to the park entrance on the right.

From the east or west via I-90 – take Exit 4 and follow the signs to I-91 north. Proceed on I-91 for 14 miles to Route 9 (Exit 19) in Northampton. Go west for

15 miles to Goshen. Turn right on Route 112 north and continue for 0.7 miles to the park entrance on the right.

From the west via Route 9 – from Dalton at the intersection with Route 8, take Route 9 west for 27 miles to Goshen. Take a left onto Route 112 and continue for 0.7 miles to the park entrance on the right.

Trail Notes

DAR State Forest is located in the foothills of the Berkshires. In 1929, the Daughters of the American Revolution (DAR) donated 1,020-acres to the Commonwealth for a state forest. Since then, 750 additional acres have been added to include the Upper and Lower Highland Lakes. There are some 15 miles of mixed-use trail through northern hardwood-conifer forest. A climb up the Goshen fire tower will give you a fantastic view of the Connecticut River Valley and into five states. The campground provides 51 wooded camp-sites, with modern comfort stations, showers, drinking water, and a private beach. Other summertime activities, besides biking, include hiking, horse-back riding, a swimming beach, and non-motorized boating.

The trails are mostly singletrack, with some areas steep and obstructed. The ride begins with a descent of over 200 feet, and then climbs steadily before descending again to the trailhead. As the trail proceeds south into the woods follow the red diamond or markers on the trees. When you get past the boat launching area, follow the blue trail markers across a dirt road and along the lake. A suggestion is to take the trail pointing to the fire tower, some 2.3 miles further. Once at the fire tower, you can take a dirt road heading south to return to the parking lot. Late spring to late fall is usually a good time to ride, but expect wet periods in the spring.

DAR State Forest

Courtesy of the Massachusetts Department of Conservation & Recreation. Photo by Kindra Clineff for the DCR©

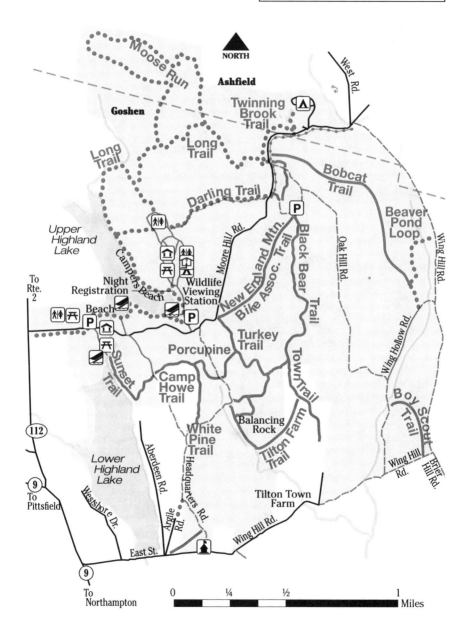

TRAIL LEGEND

- Multi-Use Bike Trail
- Hiking Trail
- Paved Road
- Unpaved Road
- Road/Highway
- Boundary Line

NORTH

Moose Run

Ashfield

Goshen

Twinning Brook Trail

West Rd.

Long Trail

Long Trail

Darling Trail

Bobcat Trail

Beaver Pond Loop

Upper Highland Lake

Moore Hill Rd.

New England Mtn. Bike Assoc. Trail

Black Bear Trail

Oak Hill Rd.

Wing Hill Rd.

Camper's Beach

Night Registration

Wildlife Viewing Station

To Rte. 2

Beach

Turkey Trail

Wing Hollow Rd.

Porcupine

Sunset Trail

Camp Howe Trail

Town Trail

Boy Scout Trail

112

White Pine Trail

Balancing Rock

Tilton Farm Trail

Lower Highland Lake

Aberdeen Rd.

Headquarters Rd.

Tilton Town Farm

Wing Hill Rd.

Bfier Hill Rd.

9

To Pittsfield

Westshore Dr.

Argile Rd.

East St.

Wing Hill Rd.

9

To Northampton

0   ¼   ½   1   Miles

Dogtown Common

Grid	C12
Length	15 miles
Surface	Singletrack, gravel roads
Setting	Woods, fire roads, rocky terrain
Difficulty	Easy to difficult
Acres	3,000
Hours	Open year round
Vicinity	Gloucester
Lat/Long	42-38/70-40 Entrance off Dogtown Road
County	Essex
Contact	Gloucester City Hall 9 Dale Avenue Gloucester, MA 01930 978-281-9782 Cape Ann Chamber of Commerce 33 Commercial Street Gloucester, MA 01930 800-321-0133
Facilities	

Getting There

Take Hwy 128 north to Gloucester. Before you get into the city limits, you'll pass over a large bridge spanning a salt water river. After crossing the bridge you will enter a large traffic circle. Follow the circle around and exit off on Route 127 towards Annisquam. Take Route 127 for a half-mile where it passes over a small bridge. Immediately after crossing the bridge, take a right onto Reynard Street. Where Reynard Street ends a quarter mile further, turn left onto Cherry Street. Look for a narrow road on your right with a small

sign for Dogtown Commons. Follow the road to the end where you will come to a gate and cannot go further. This is where you park your car.

Trail Notes

Dogtown is located on Cape Ann, about 30 miles southwest of Boston, now a summer vacation area near Rockport and Gloucester. It was first settled in colonial days. The early settlers tried to farm the land, but with difficulty because of the rocky terrain. Eventually the wealthier residents migrated to the coastline to take up fishing and trading, and the vacated houses became inhabited by vagrants and social outcasts in the 18th century. Many of the widows of sea-goers and soldiers who never returned kept dogs for protection. As these last inhabitants died their pets became wild, roaming the moors in packs, and thus Dogtown acquired its name. By 1830 the village was deserted. The land was eventually purchased by the wealthy William Babson. His grandson, financier and philanthropist Roger Babson, commissioned local stonecutters to carve inspirational sayings into the boulders in the area during the Great Depression. They can be found today on the Babson Boulder Trail. Their sayings are as applicable today and they were then – "Courage", "Ideas", "Get a Job", "Never Try Never Win", and many more. Upon his death he donated the land to the town of Gloucester.

Most of the Dogtown area is now dense woodland, bisected and crisscrossed by trails and roads. These trails are a mix of smooth doubletrack fire roads, grassy doubletrack trails, and singletrack. The terrain is rolling, with frequent short climbs and descents. Many of the singletrack trails east of Peter's Pulpit, on the eastern side of Dogtown, are laden with rocks and hardly passable. A lot of the trails are easy paths, but not recommended for the first time cyclist, as these trails are often unmarked, confusing, and where one can easily find themselves lost in the maze. But if you do become lost, you are never more than a mile or so from Route 127, as it completely circles the Dogtown Reservation. The woods are divided by a railroad track, which you must cross or ride to get from one side of the trail to another. Horseback riding is popular in Dogtown, so be courteous and try not to startle a horse when you pass.

Dogtown Common (continued)

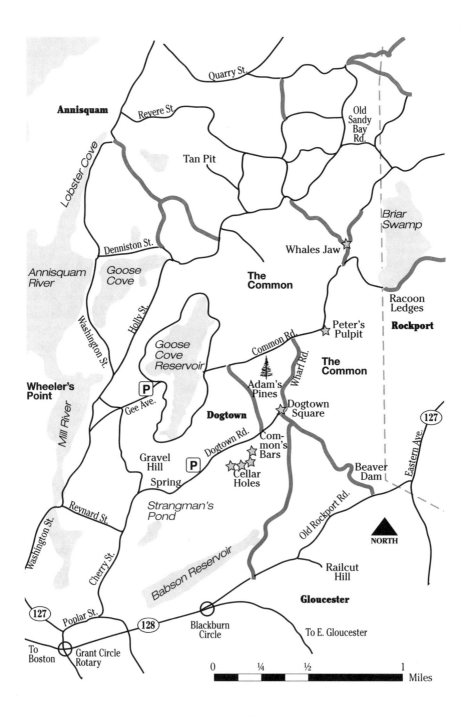

Douglas State Forest

Grid	E7
Length	30 miles
Surface	Singletrack, dirt and gravel roads
Setting	Woods, rocky
Difficulty	Easy to difficult
Acres	5,730
Fees	None, unless you park in the picnic area
Hours	Half hour before dawn to a half hour after sunset
Vicinity	Douglas
Lat/Long	42-03/71-47 Trailhead off Route 16
County	Worcester
Contact	Douglas State Forest 107 Wallum Lake Road Douglas, MA 01516 508-476-7872
Facilities	P [symbols]

Getting There

From the east or west take I-90 to Route 395 (Exit 10). Follow Route 395 south to Route 16 (Exit 2), and proceed east for 6 miles to Cedar Street. Turn right on Cedar Street and go 0.5 miles to Wallum Lake Road. Continue on Wallum Lake Road for 1-mile, following the signs to Douglas State Forest. When you are in the forest you come to a 'Y' in the road. Keep to the right and park in the upper lot.

Trail Notes

Douglas State Forest is located on the southern border of central Massachusetts. It offers a variety of recreational opportunities besides biking, including swimming, hiking, horseback riding, and cross-country skiing. Facilities include drinking water, restrooms, a pavilion, bathhouses, swimming beach, interpretive center, picnic area, and boat ramps. Drinking water and restrooms are only available in the picnic area, and only during the summer season. Among the features of the forest are Wallum Lake and a rare Atlantic White Cedar swamp, of which 5 acres is designated as a 'Massachusetts Wildland'. It can be accessed via a boardwalk trail. Be aware that the forest is open to hunters during hunting season, except on Sundays.

There are over 30 miles of trail and dirt roads. The trail are limited to non-motorized use, and with the exception of a few trails limited to hiking in the southeastern corner, all are open to mountain biking. The forest sits on a plateau, and there are no major hills. Many of the singletrack trails are quite rocky, and they frequently intersect with loose gravel forest roads and double-track woods roads.

Leave No Trace

Ride only on existing trails. Never create new trails including short cuts and "turn-outs" around fallen logs, water bars, and muddy areas. Ride through puddles rather than around them. Avoid soft and wet trails.

When slowing, modulate brakes-both front and back to prevent skidding and rutting of trails.

TRAIL LEGEND

———————	Multi-Use Bike Trail
‒ ▬ ▬ ▬ ▬ ▬	Midstate Trail
• • • • • • • • • • •	Hiking Trail
▬ ▬ ▬ ▬ ▬ ▬ ▬	SNETT Trail
———————	Paved Road
▬▬▬▬▬▬▬▬	Unpaved Road
———————	Road/Highway
·•·•·•·•·•·	Power/Pipe Line
– – – – – –	Boundary Line

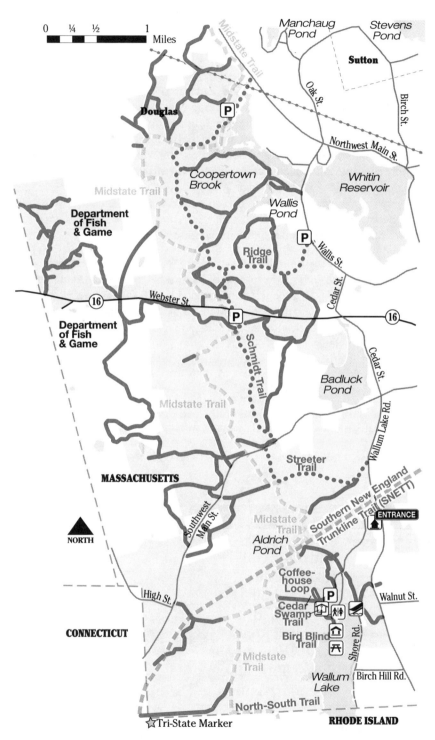

Douglas State Forest

Courtesy of the Massachusetts Department of Conservation and Recreation. Photo by Kindra Clineff for the DCR©

Emerald Necklace

Grid	D10
Length	6 miles (16 miles including the on-road loop)
Surface	Paved
Setting	Parks, urban
Difficulty	Easy
Acres	1,100-acre chain of parks
Vicinity	Boston
Lat/Long	41-19/71-07 Trail at Jamical Pond
County	Suffolk
Contact	Boston Visitor's Bureau (Visitors Information section) 617-536-4100
Facilities	

Getting There
From Storrow Drive, take Arlington Street to the traffic lights, then left a short distance to the Public Garden on the left. Parking is available at the Boston Common Underground Parking Garage. Take a left onto Boylston Street, then left again at the next trail light onto Charles Street and the parking garage entrance on the right.

Trail Notes
Emerald Necklace is a long stretch of park space stretching from Boston's Back Bay to Franklin Park, and was created between 1878 and 1896 by landscape artist Frederick Law Olmstead. He was best known for his work designing Central Park in New York. The project began with the effort to clean up and control the marshy area, which became the Back Bay and the Fens. Olmstead proposed that the Muddy River, which flowed from Jamaica Pond into the Fens, be included in the park plan. The river's current was

dredged into a winding stream and directed into the Charles River. The corridor encompassing the river became a linear park.

The parks are almost contiguous with one another and are irregularly-shaped according to whatever land was available at the time. The six parks in the Emerald Necklace – The Back Bay Fens, Riverway, Olmsted Park, Jamaica Park, Arnold Arboretum and Franklin Park – stretch for 7 miles from the Charles River to Dorchester.

Points of interest near the Emerald Necklace include:

Isabella Stewart Gardner Museum   Massachusetts College of Art
Museum of Fine Arts   Massachusetts State House
Emerson College   Simmons College
Emmanuel College   Symphony Hall
Fenway Park   Wentworth Institute of Technology
Franklin Park Zoo   Wheelock College
Landmark Center

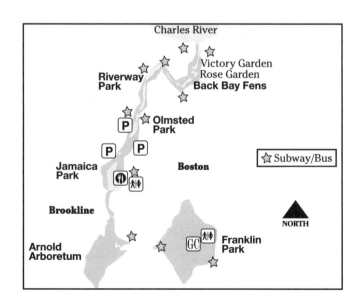

Emerald Necklace (continued)

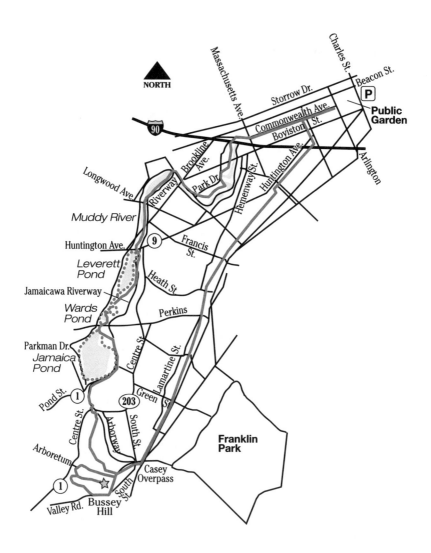

Erving State Forest

Grid	C5
Length	20 miles
Surface	Singletrack, doubletrack, logging & fire roads
Setting	Deep woods, ponds, Laurel Lake
Difficulty	Easy to moderate, some more difficult
Acres	4,500
Fees	$5.00 vehicle fee
Hours	Dawn to 7:30 pm
Vicinity	Erving, Warwick
Lat/Long	42-37/72-22 Trailhead at Laurel Lake
County	Franklin
Contact	Erving State Forest 200 East Main Street Erving, MA 01344 978-544-3939
Facilities	

Getting There

From the north – Take I-91 south to Route 2 east (Exit 27) to Erving. Turn left at the fire station onto Church Street (becomes North Street). Go 0.9 miles and turn right on Swamp Road. The contact station is located 1.5 miles on the right.

From the south – Take I-91 north to Route 2 east (Exit 27) to Erving. Follow directions from the north.

Erving State Forest (continued)

From the west – Take Route 2 east to Erving. Follow direction from the north.

From the east – Take Route 2 west to Erving, then left on Route 2A (east of Main Street). Continue 0.7 miles and then turn left on Moss Brook Road. Go 1.9 mile and bear left on Quarry Road. The park entrance is on the left.

Trail Notes

Erving State Forest is located in Midwestern Massachusetts by the Berkshires, in the towns of Erving and Warwick. The trails consist of logging roads, woodland doubletrack and singletrack. There is a one-mile loop trail that begins at the contact station and takes you to an overlook with a dramatic view of Mount Monadnock in New Hampshire. The 51-acre Laurel Lake has a sandy beach and stone-terraced gardens. The forest offers a rich diversity of trees and woodland flora.

Starting your ride through the campground from the Laurel Lake parking lot takes you to a couple of old woods roads leading south. This route provides some good terrain with easier uphill climbs and more difficult downhills. Warwick and Northfield State Forests border Erving north of Laurel Lake. Their woods roads range in difficulty from maintained dirt roads to double and singletrack paths.

NEMBA

The New England Mountain Bike Association is a non-profit organization dedicated to promoting sustainable trail access for mountain bicyclist, and to maintaining the trails on which mountain biker ride. NEMBA supports the conservation of open spaces and is committed to educating mountain bicyclists to ride sensitively and responsibly in order to protect the natural environment and the experience of other trail users.

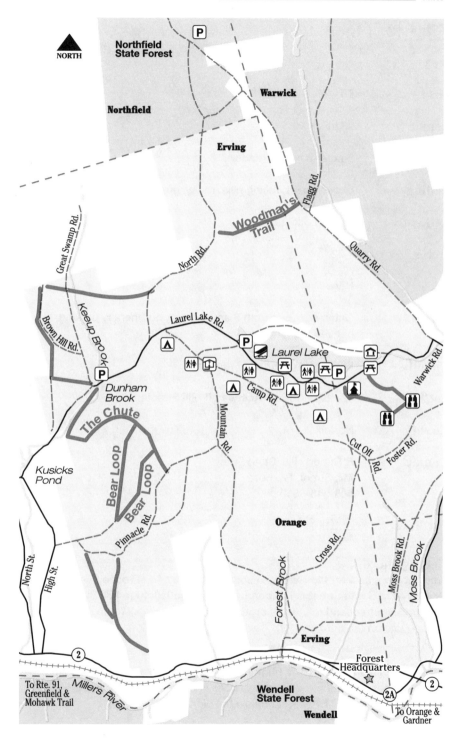

NORTH

Northfield State Forest

Warwick

Northfield

Erving

Great Swamp Rd.

Woodman's Trail

Flagg Rd.

North Rd.

Quarry Rd.

Keeup Brook

Laurel Lake Rd.

Brown Hill Rd.

Laurel Lake

Warwick Rd.

Dunham Brook

Camp Rd.

The Chute

Kusicks Pond

Bear Loop

Mountain Rd.

Bear Loop

Cut Off Rd.

Foster Rd.

Pinnacle Rd.

Orange

Cross Rd.

North St.

High St.

Forest Brook

Moss Brook Rd.

Moss Brook

Erving

Forest Headquarters

2

To Rte. 91, Greenfield & Mohawk Trail

Millers River

Wendell State Forest

2A

2

To Orange & Gardner

Wendell

69

F. Gilbert Hills State Forest

Grid	E9
Length	23 miles
Surface	Singletrack, dirt roads
Setting	Dense forest, rolling hills, rocky, gravely
Difficulty	Easy to difficult
Acres	1,027
Fees	None
Hours	Gates are open from 8 am to 5 pm, but there is parking outside the gates
Vicinity	Foxboro, Wrentham, Franklin
Lat/Long	42-03/71-16 Access off Mill Street
County	Norfolk
Contact	F. Gilbert Hills State Forest Mill Street, Foxboro 508-543-5850
Facilities	P 🏕 🚰

Getting There

From Boston, take I-93 to I-95, then south to Route 140. Proceed west on Route 140 to South Street in Foxborough, then south (left) to Mill Street. Go right on Mill Street and follow the brown state forest signs. You will find forest parking lots on the right and left. The parking lot on the left is not gated at dusk.

From I-495, take Route 1 (Exit 14) north to Thurston Street. Take a left (Thurston becomes West Street in Foxboro) pass Normandy Farms campground, and then left onto Mill Street and follow the signs.

Trail Notes

The F. Gilbert Hills State Forest is located in southeastern Massachusetts. The forest is divided into three sections, Foxboro, Wrentham, and Franklin. Each refers to the town that it's in, with Wrentham probably the more technical, Foxboro the more populated, and Franklin the less utilized. There are some 23 miles of trails looping through the forest. One of these leads to the Warner Trail, a long distance trail through Norfolk County on its way to Rhode Island. Mountain biking is a popular activity in the forest, providing some of the best riding experiences in the area. The woodlands are densely forested with a maze of trails among a variety of hardwood trees. The gravelly earth and rock, derived from past glaciers, tend to be well drained and rarely muddy. The dense woods provide plenty of shade, with some great scenery, and challenging elevation changes.

These trails range from old jeep roads and rough dirt roads to miles of smooth to difficult singletrack with steep climbs over loose rock and sandy slopes to tight downhills. Most of the trails are open to mountain bikers, hikers, horseback riders, and motorcyclists, with the exception of some sections of the hiking trails.

TRAIL LEGEND

▬▬▬▬▬	Multi-Use Bike Trail
▬ ▬ ▬ ▬ ▬	Warner Trail
•••••••••‹	Hiking Trail
▪▪▪▪▪▪▪▪▪	Equestrian Trail
▪▪▪▪▪▪▪▪▪▪▪	MB/Motorcycle Trail
▬▬▬▬▬	Paved Road
▬ ▬ ▬ ▬ ▬	Unpaved Road
▬▬▬▬▬	Road/Highway
‑ ‑ ‑ ‑ ‑	Boundary Line

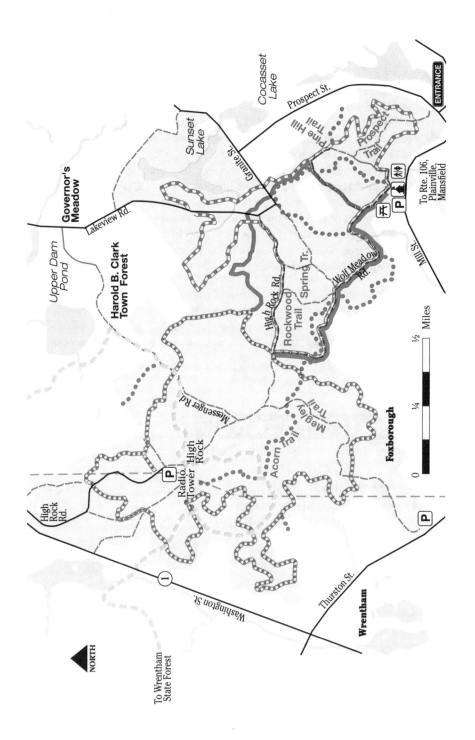

Freetown-Fall River State Forest

Grid	F10
Length	50 miles
Surface	Singletrack, dirt & gravel roads
Setting	Woods, rocky, steep hills
Difficulty	Easy to difficult
Acres	10,000
Hours	Dawn to dusk
Vicinity	Freetown
Lat/Long	41-47/71/03 Slab Bridge & Payne road
County	Bristol
Contact	Freetown-Fall River State Forest
	Stab Bridge Road
	Assonet, MA
	508-644-5522
Facilities	

Getting There

From Boston, take I-93 south to Hwy 24, then south to South Main Street (Exit 10). Bear left onto South Main Street. Turn left at four corners onto Route 79 north and then right onto Elm Street (becomes Slab Bridge Road). Continue for 1.5-miles to the forest entrance and parking on the left.

Trail Notes

Freetown State Forest is located in southeast Massachusetts. The Forest is a vast track of land with many miles of unpaved roads and trails. Near the main entrance is a day use area, with restrooms, picnic area, a wading pool and play fields. The Forest is popular, but this is a very remote area, so bring a map and get directions. Additional facilities include a wading pool, pavilion, and a sports field. Motorcycles must be properly registered.

Freetown-Fall River State Forest (continued)

Profile Rock, a 50-foot outcropping, shows a profile of what the Wampanoag Indians believe to be Chief Massasoit. The Forest includes the 227-acre Watuppa Reservation, which belongs to the Wampanoag Nation, and is the site of annual tribal meetings.

The soil, stone laden and gravelly, tends to drain quickly, allowing you to avoid mud slicks and bogs, even after a rainstorm. Motorized vehicles are allowed, which has degraded a lot of the dirt roads. You'll find many of the singletracks difficult riding. They tend to be tight and twisty, with large rocky sections. The surface often changes quickly, from flat and smooth to fields of large rocks. There are also a lot of elevation changes on some of the trails, such as the steep series of hills at Copicut Street, not far from the train tracks. These singletrack trails are connected and bisected with fire roads, which help to keep you oriented. There are also signs noting the direction of primary locations.

TRAIL LEGEND	
───────	Multi-Use Trail
▬ ▬ ▬ ▬ ▬	Long Trail
●●●●●●●●●●	Hiking Trail
───────	Paved Road
▬▬▬▬▬▬	Unpaved Road
───────	Road/Highway
++++++++++	Railroad Tracks
•••••••••	Power/Pipe Line
─ ─ ─ ─ ─	Boundary Line

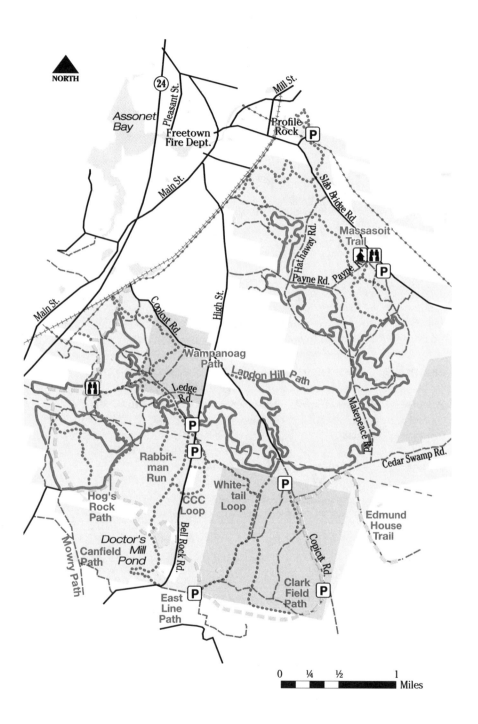

NORTH

Assonet
Bay

Pleasant St.

24

Mill St.

Profile
Rock

P

Freetown
Fire Dept.

Main St.

Slab Bridge Rd.

Massasoit
Trail

P

Hathaway Rd.

Payne Rd. Payne

Main St.

Copicut Rd.

High St.

Wampanoag
Path

Landon Hill Path

Ledge
Rd.

Makepeace Rd.

P

Cedar Swamp Rd.

P

Rabbit-
man
Run

White-
tail
Loop

P

Hog's
Rock
Path

CCC
Loop

Edmund
House
Trail

Doctor's
Canfield Mill
Path Pond

Bell Rock Rd.

Copicut Rd.

Clark
Field
Path

P

Mowry Path

P

East
Line
Path

0   ¼   ½   1
Miles

Georgetown-Rowley State Park

Grid	C11
Length	20 miles
Surface	Singtletrack, gravel roads
Setting	Relatively flat, some climbs
Difficulty	Easy to moderate
Acres	1,112
Fees	None
Hours	Sunrise to sunset
Vicinity	Georgetown
Lat/Long	42-43/70-59 Entrance off Pingree Farm Road
County	Essex
Contact	Georgetown-Rowley State Forest Route 97 Georgetown, MA 978-887-5931
Facilities	P

Getting There
From Boston take I-93 north to I-95. From I-95 take the Georgetown exit (Route 133) into Georgetown Center. Turn left (south) onto Route 97. After passing a cemetery, turn left onto East Street. Follow East Street to a T at Pingree Farm Road. Go left on Pingree Farm Road, and then right to the Forest entrance and a small dirt parking lot at the end of the road.

Trail Notes

Georgetown-Rowley State Forest is located in northeastern Massachusetts, between the towns of Georgetown and Rowley about 30 miles north of Boston. All services are available in Georgetown, including a bike shop. A feature of the woods is the well-preserved stone walls built by early settlers before being abandoned as they took up fishing and trading or moved to the rockless Midwest. You can also link up with the adjoining Willowdale and Bradley Palmer State Parks to the southeast. Hunting is allowed, and the seasons are posted on signs at the trailhead.

The trails run through deep woods of oak and pine, wetlands, and a working horse farm at the northern edge of the forest. Although relatively flat, you will find all types of terrain, from wide, gravel trails to tight and rocky singletrack, with some short steep climbs and descents. The trails can get muddy with standing water at times after heavy rains. Many of the trails run off a main fire road that goes from the trailhead into Rowley and Route 133. The singletrack trails are maintained by NEMBA. They are marked with light blue rings on the trees.

Georgetown-Rowley State Park

Courtesy of the Massachusetts Department of Conservation and Recreation. Photo by Fred Popper for the DCR©

Georgetown-Rowley
State Park (continued)

TRAIL LEGEND

───────	Multi-Use Bike Trail
··········	Hiking Trail
‑ ‑ ‑ ‑ ‑	Unpaved Road
───────	Road/Highway
‑ ‑ ‑ ‑ ‑	Boundary Line

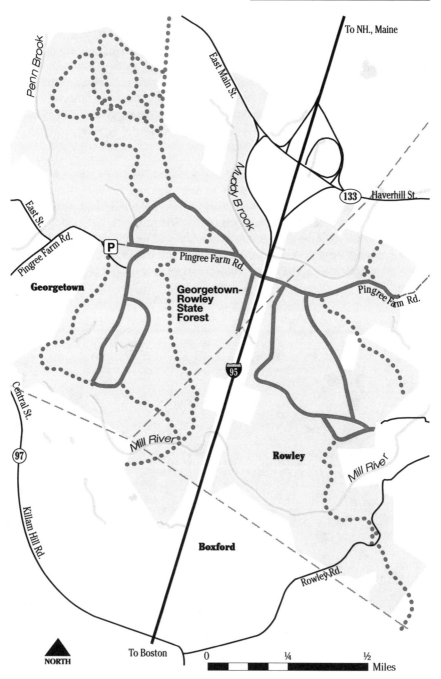

Penn Brook

East Main St.

To NH., Maine

Muddy Brook

East St.

Pingree Farm Rd.

P

Pingree Farm Rd.

133 Haverhill St.

Pingree Farm Rd.

Georgetown

Georgetown-Rowley State Forest

95

Rowley

Central St.

97

Mill River

Mill River

Killam Hill Rd.

Boxford

Rowley Rd.

NORTH

To Boston

0	¼	½

Miles

Great Brook Farm State Park

Grid	C9
Length	20 miles
Surface	Doubletrack, singletrack
Setting	Relatively flat, a few hills, working daily farm
Difficulty	Easy to moderate
Acres	995
Fees	Parking
Vicinity	Carlisle
Lat/Long	42-34/71-21 Entrance off North Road
County	Middlesex
Contact	Great Brook Farm State Farm 984 Lowell Road Carlisle, MA 01741 978-369-6312
Facilities	

Getting There

From Route 128, take Route 225 (Exit 31B) west for 8 miles to the Carlisle center rotary. Turn right onto Lowell Street (following the sign to Chelmsford). The Park entrance is 2 miles further on the right, and the park office is located at 964 Lowell Street, just beyond the entrance. Make a right turn onto North Road. The parking area is a half-mile further on the right.

From the north take Route 495 south to Route 110 (Exit 34). Follow Route 110 west for 6 miles to Chelmsford center, continue through a 4-way stop onto Route 4 south for 1 mile. Take a right fork onto Concord Road towards Carlisle. The park office is 2 miles ahead on the left. Just beyond the office is the entrance on the right. The park is just beyond the office. Go left on North Road for a half mile to the parking area on the left.

Great Brook Farm State Park (continued)

From the south, take Route 495 north to Westford & Route 225 (Exit 32). At the bottom of the ramp go right. At the T intersection go left onto Route 225. Continue on Route 225 to Carlisle center. Take Lowell Street toward Chelmsford. The entrance to the park is 2 miles further on the right and the Park Office is just beyond, also on the right

Trail Notes

The farm and buildings at Great Brook Farm comprise a classic eastern Massachusetts agricultural landscape. This is an active dairy farm operating year-round and guided barn tours, including a few barnyard animals, are available from May to October. The setting is one of meadows, pastures, ponds, diversified woodlands and historic structures that serve as reminders of our agricultural past.

There is a variety of trail in the park, and they are signed as to use. Most of the trails are open to biking. Many of these trails are wide, level doubletrack and not rutted, attracting family groups. The singletracks route you around the perimeters of meadows and pastures, and are generally easy. The Wood Chuck loop trail does provide some larger hills.

A convenient starting point is from the Hart Barn Ski Center. The trail will cross several bridges, coming eventually to a cabin on the right. Left of the area, you can find some of the ruins of homes in the nearby woods. The Litchfield Loop Trail takes you to a paved road, which crosses over to a canoe launch. From there you can take the Pine Point Loop Trail, or the Beaver Loop trail which spurs to the right. The Beaver Loop trail leads you to a pleasant picnic area by Meadow Pond. The Pine Point loop takes you across a bridge into a field. Go through the trail to the gates in front of the road. Take a left before the gate and continue through the woods towards the right and eventually you will cross the road back to the cornfield near the parking lot. Turn left at the cornfield to work your way back to the Ski Center.

Trail (miles)	Marking
Pine Point Loop (2.0)	Pine tree
Woodchuck Trail (1.5)	Paw print
Litchfield Loop (1.0)	Maple leaf
Acorn Trail (3.0)	Acorn
Lantern Loop (1.0)	Hiker symbol
Heartbreak Ridge (2.0)	Blank blue marker
Tophet Loop (1.0)	Hiker symbol
Maple Ridge (.5)	Blank blue marker
Fern Loop (1.0)	

TRAIL LEGEND

- ———— Multi-Use Bike Trail
- ·━·━·━· Paved Road Trail
- ········· Alternate Trail
- ‑‑‑‑‑‑‑‑ Unpaved Road
- ———— Road/Highway
- – – – – Boundary Line

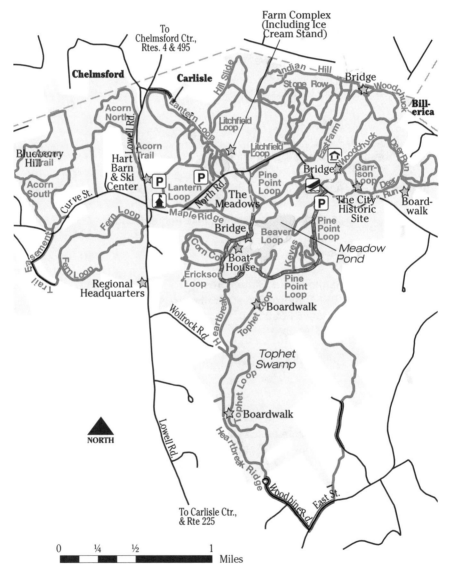

Farm Complex
(Including Ice
Cream Stand)

To
Chelmsford Ctr.,
Rtes. 4 & 495

Chelmsford **Carlisle**

Indian Hill

Hill Slide

Stone Row

Bridge

Woodchuck

Bill-erica

Acorn North

Litchfield Loop

Litchfield Loop

East Farm

Woodchuck

Deer Run

Blueberry Hill Trail

Acorn Trail

Hart Barn & Ski Center

Acorn South

Curve St.

Lantern Loop

Acorn Trail

Lowell Rd.

P

P

Lantern Loop

North Rd.

The Meadows

Pine Point Loop

Bridge

Garrison Loop

Deer Run

P

"The City" Historic Site

Board-walk

Fern Loop

Maple Ridge

Bridge

Beaver Loop

Pine Point Loop

Meadow Pond

Fern Loop

Trail Easement

Corn Cob

Boat-House

Erickson Loop

Keyes Loop

Regional Headquarters

Wolfrock Rd.

Heartbreak Ridge

Tophet Loop

Pine Point Loop

Boardwalk

Tophet Swamp

Tophet Loop

▲
NORTH

Lowell Rd.

Boardwalk

Heartbreak Ridge

Woodbine Rd.

East St.

To Carlisle Ctr.,
& Rte 225

0   ¼   ½   1
Miles

Harold Parker State Forest

Grid	C10
Length	35 miles
Surface	Singletrack, fire roads
Setting	Rolling hills, swampy areas, rock outcrops
Difficulty	Easy to difficult
Acres	3,000
Fees	Camping & swimming area
Vicinity	Andover
Lat/Long	42-38/71-04 Route 114 & Parker Road
County	Essex
Contact	Harold Parker State Forest 1951 Turnpike Street, Route 114 North Andover, MA 01810 978-686-3391
Facilities	

Getting There

From Boston, take Hwy 93 north to Route 125 north (Exit 41) toward Andover. Go about 4 miles to the State Police Barracks on the right. Turn right on Harold Parker Road to Jenkins Road. Turn left on Jenkins Road, then right onto Middleton. Continue for about 1.5 miles to a parking lot on the left.

From Lawrence, take I-495 to Route 114 (Exit 42). Go east for 6 miles to a brown State Forest sign. Turn right and proceed to the end of the road. The forest headquarters is on your left.

Trail Notes

Located about 20 miles north of Boston, the Harold Parker State Forest lies in Andover, North Andover, North Reading, and Middleton. The forest consists

of rolling hills, low lying swampy areas, rock outcrops, and several ponds. Its 3,000 plus acres of woods are predominately Central Hardwood Hemlock and White Pine. The topography was created by past glaciers, as evidenced today by glacial erratics. The Pentacook Indians were inhabiting the area around the time English farmers began settling there in the 1600 hundreds. Agriculture was finally abandoned by the mid-nineteenth century and the forest began to renew itself. You can still find remnants of an 18th century sawmill and homesteads.

The 35 miles of logging roads and trails offer quiet seclusion for off-road recreation. Opportunities, in addition to mountain biking, include hiking, horseback riding, swimming, fishing, hunting, camping, picnicking, and non-motorized boating. There are no bike rental, horse, or boat rentals available at the facility. The campground is located about 2 miles from forest headquarters on Jenkins Road. Electric and water hookups are not available, but there are bathrooms with hot water showers, picnic tables and grills. Berry Pond, the day use area, is open from Memorial Day to Labor Day. It has a sand beach and washhouse with flush toilets and changing stalls, and there are lifeguards on duty.

The double and single track trails cut through deep woods, grassy wetlands, and around several ponds and granite outcroppings. The woods roads tend to be easy, while the more challenging trails are moderate to difficult. Paved roads connect the loops and networks of trails. Some of the woods trails have short spur trails branching off that end at private property. Just double back! Two other nearby areas for mountain biking are the easier Bradley Palmer State Park and the more difficult Georgetown-Rowley State Forest.

Harold Parker State Forest

Courtesy of the Massachusetts Department of Conservation & Recreation. Photo by Kindra Clineff for the DCR©

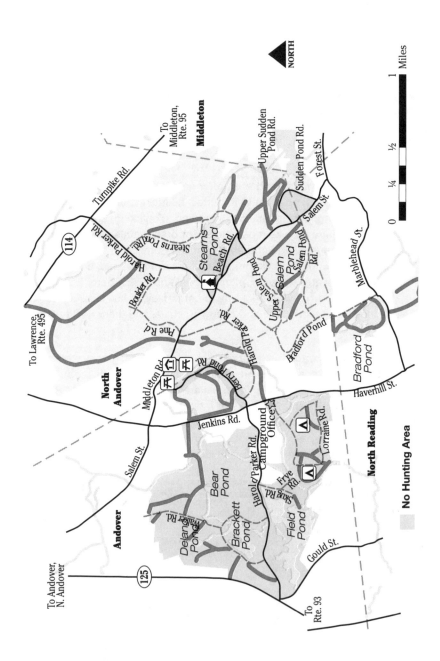

Holyoke Range State Park

Grid	D5
Length	15 miles
Surface	Doubletrack, singletrack, park roads
Setting	Woods, hills, rocky areas
Difficulty	Moderate to difficult
Acres	3,000
Hours	Dawn to one-half hour after dusk
Vicinity	Amherst
Lat/Long	42-19/72-29 Trailhead off Bay Road
County	Hampshire
Contact	Holyoke Range State Park Route 116 Amherst, MA 01002 413-586-0350 Visitors Center 413-253-2883
Facilities	

Getting There

From I-91, go east on Route 9 for less than a mile, cross the Connecticut River, then east (right) to Bay Road to Route 116. There are two trailheads into the park. To get to the southern one, continue on Route 116 past the Visitor Center for one mile, then turn left on Amherst Street toward Route 202 for about a half mile. At Bachelor Street turn left for 0.6 miles to a brown gate and trailhead parking.

To get to the northern trailhead, stay on Bay Road (instead on turning onto Route 116) for 1.3 miles to a sign "Holyoke Range Conservation Area" at a small turnoff on the right. You can park at the Visitor Center. It is suggested you ask how best to go from there.

Trail Notes

Holyoke Range State Park stretches from Hadley to Belchertown on a 7-mile ridge that towers above the surrounding miles of flat farmlands. The ridge rises to 1,000 feet in elevation, providing scenic panoramic views easily accessible by mountain bike. The park is mostly wooded, consisting of birch-beech-hemlock on the north side and oak-hickory on the south, corresponding to the east-west orientation of the ridgeline. Adding to the diversity are streams, ponds, wetlands, and thickets. The ridge is a patchwork of state, town and private lands. The Notch Visitor Center, located on Route 116 in Amherst, is open between Friday and Tuesday from 8am to 4pm.

The trails are mostly doubletrack and challenging, with rolling terrain and long climbs, sometimes steep and rocky. The southern access is a variety of loop trails, combining the easier Lower Access with the Upper Access, Southside, Swamp and a short mountain bike trail cutoff. The northern access is a 2.5 miles loop combining the Robert Frost and Northside trails. You can connect to these two trails from the southern access via the Southside or Swamp trails.

TRAIL LEGEND	
————————	Multi-Use Bike Trail
- - - - - - -	M-M Trail
- - - - - - - -	Unpaved Road
————————	Road/Highway
+++++++++	Power/Pipe Line
– – – – –	Boundary Line

Trail Names

AC (yellow) Amherst Conservation	Ns (blue) Northside
Bb (yellow) Brookbank	PT Pond Trail
Cb (blue) Ken Cuddebank	PW Pete's Wicked
Cs (red) Cliffside	RC Roller Coaster
Ho (blue) Hollow	RF (orange) Robert Frost
JL Jacob's Ladder	SA (yellow) Sweet Alice
Lk (red) Link	Sp Serpentine
LL (blue) Laurel Loop	Ss (blue) Southside
M-M (white) Metacomet-Monadnock	Sw (red) Swamp
	Tw Twister

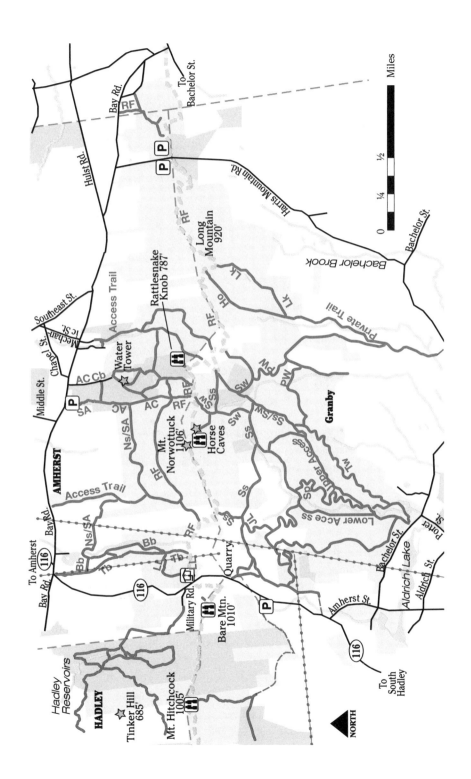

NORTH

Miles

0   ¼   ½

To Bachelor St.

Bay Rd.   RF

Hulst Rd.

P P

P

Harris Mountain Rd.

Bachelor St.

Long Mountain 920'

RF

Bachelor Brook

Southeast St.

Access Trail

Rattlesnake Knob 787'

RF

Lk

Ho

Lk

Private Trail

Water Tower

Mechanic St.

Chapel St.

Middle St.

AC Cb

P

SA

AC   Ns/SA

AC   RF/

Mt. Norwottuck 1106'

Horse Caves

Ms/Ss

Sw

Md

Sw

Pw

Granby

AMHERST

Access Trail

RF

Ns/SA

Ms/Sw

Ss

Tw

Upper Access

Bay Rd.

To Amherst 116

Bb

Ns/SA

Bb   Tb

Bb   Tb

116

Military Rd.

Bare Mtn. 1010'

Quarry

Ss

Ss

Jl   Ss

Lower Access

Sps

Jl

P

Bachelor St.

Porter St.

Aldrich Lake

Aldrich St.

Amherst St.

116

To South Hadley

Hadley Reservoirs

HADLEY

Tinker Hill 685'

Mt. Hitchcock 1005'

Kenneth Debuque State Forest

Grid	C3
Length	35 miles
Surface	Forest roads, singletrack
Setting	Deep woods, hills, small lakes
Difficulty	Easy to difficult
Acres	7,882
Hours	Sunrise to sunset
Vicinity	Hawley
Lat/Long	42-33/72-57 Hallockville Pond
County	Franklin
Contact	Kenneth Dubuque Memorial State Forest Route 8A Hawley, MA 413-339-5504
Facilities	P

Getting There
From Route 2, go about 5 miles south on Route 8A to forest headquarters. Forest headquarters is about a half mile north of the junctions of Routes 116 and 8A.

From Route 115 in Plainfield, take Route 8A for one mile to the Hallockville Pond/Student Conservation Association entrance on the left to the parking area.

Trail Notes
Kenneth Dubuque State Forest is located in the northern Berkshires in western Massachusetts, within Hawley, Plainfield and Savoy. The forest consists

of hardwood and spruce-fir with some 35 miles of mixed-use trails. Points of interest include the abandoned village of South Hawley, remains of a mill complex at Hallockville Pond, a fieldstone "beehive" charcoal kiln, and Moody Springs. There are no services available, so your trash is carry-in, carry-out.

There are lots of hills, and the trails are mostly doubletrack, with a few long singletracks. The majority of the riding is in the eastern part of the forest. Many of the singletracks are located north of Hallockville Road in the center of the forest. The usual place to start is from forest headquarters. This will take you uphill on Klingholt Road, passing through a metal forest gate to an abandoned apple orchard. By bearing up a field to your left, your will come to an old jeep road. Off that road you have a number of riding options. You will probably need a map to keep yourself oriented. Because of changing riding conditions, trails sometimes don't exist on the map, while others no longer exist even though still shown on the map. Be aware that some of the roads and trails take you beyond the forest boundaries.

The DCR's Division of State Parks and Recreation
This Division is responsible for the maintenance and management of over 430,000 acres of privately and state-owned forest and parks, nearly 10% of the Commonwealth's total land mass. Within the lands managed by the Division of State Parks and Recreation are some 29 campgrounds, over 2,000 miles of trails, 87 beaches, 37 swimming, wading, and spray pools, 62 campgrounds, 55 ballfields, and 145 miles of paved bike and rail trails.

TRAIL LEGEND

————————	Multi-Use Bike Trail
– – – – – –	Multi-Use (Winter)
————————	Paved Road
– – – – – – –	Unpaved Road
– – – – – –	Boundary Line

Kenneth Debuque State Forest (continued)

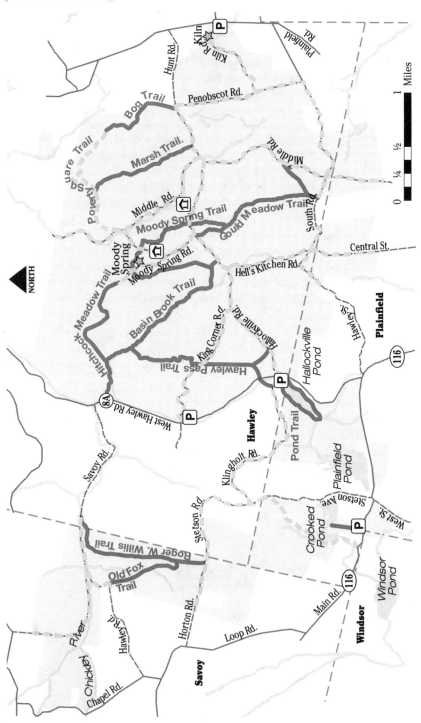

Leominster State Forest

Grid	C7
Length	20 miles
Surface	Unpaved fire roads, singletrack
Setting	Deep woods, rolling hills, ponds, rocky areas
Difficulty	Moderate
Acres	4,300
Fees	Parking lot fee between Memorial Day and Labor Day on paved parking lots
Hours	Sunrise to sunset
Vicinity	Fitchburg, Leominster. Westminster
Lat/Long	42-31/71-51 Rocky Pond Road entrance
County	Worcester
Contact	Leominster State Forest 90 Fitchburg Road, Route 31 Westminster, MA 01473 978-874-2303
Facilities	[P] [♦♦] [⛱] [🍴] [🏊]

Getting There

From Boston go west on Route 2 to Route 31 (Fitchburg), then south and past the Forest Headquarters to Rocky Pond Road and a parking area.

From the Worcester area take Route 190 north to Route 140 North (Exit 5). At Route 31 continue north to Rocky Pond Road and the parking area.

Leominster State Forest (continued)

Trail Notes

Leominster State Forest is located in north-central Massachusetts. In the early 1700's land grants were given to the heirs of solders killed in the French and Indian Wars. These parcels became known as Notown. In 1938 the lands of Notown, almost all of which is part of Leominster State Forest, were incorporated in the towns of Leominster, Fitchburg, Westminster, and Princeton. Some of the cellar holes, stonewalls and fruit trees are still visible along the forest roads and trails. There is a swimming beach, picnic tables, and a bathhouse at Crow Hill Pond. Other activities include kayaking, canoeing, fishing, and hunting in season. The forest has no camping facilities. Drinking water is available in season. Interpretive programs are offered from Memorial Day to Labor Day. The hills are lined with birch, elm and oak trees, plus bushes such as ferns and mountain laurel. As an interesting side trip visit the town of Leominster, home to the National Plastic Center and Museum.

The trails range from rolling unpaved fire roads to more technical, singletrack, multi-use trails. The hiking trails are off limits to bikers. The trails connect several rugged woods roads through scenic and peaceful woodland. Hazards include boulders, loose soil, eroded sections, and occasional standing water after heavy rains. You will also experience some steep but short riding changes and some long climbs that will test your stamina. North of Rock Pond Road you'll find many of the winding singletrack trails. A popular sport in Leominster State Forest is rock climbing.

Leominster State Forest.

Courtesy of the Massachusetts Departments of Conservation and Recreation. Photo from the DCR.

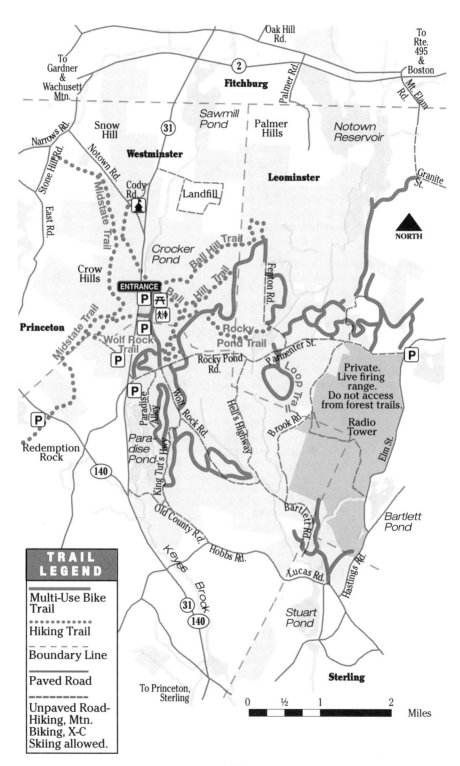

To Gardner & Wachusett Mtn.

Oak Hill Rd.

To Rte. 495 & Boston

2

Fitchburg

Palmer Rd.

Mt. Elam Rd.

Narrows Rd.

Snow Hill

31

Sawmill Pond

Palmer Hills

Notown Reservoir

Stone Hill Rd.

Notown Rd.

Westminster

Leominster

Granite St.

East Rd.

Cody Rd.

Landfill

Midstate Trail

Ball Hill Trail

Crocker Pond

NORTH

Crow Hills

Fenton Rd.

ENTRANCE

P

Princeton

Ball Hill Trail

Midstate Trail

P

Wolf Rock Trail

P

Rocky Pond Trail

Parmenter St.

P

Rocky Pond Rd.

Private. Live firing range. Do not access from forest trails.

P

Paradise Alley

Wolf Rock Rd.

Hell's Highway

Loop Trail

Radio Tower

Elm St.

P

Redemption Rock

Para-dise Pond

King Tut's Hwy

Brook Rd.

140

Old County Rd.

Hobbs Rd.

Bartlett Rd.

Bartlett Pond

Keyes Brook

31

140

Lucas Rd.

Hastings Rd.

Stuart Pond

Sterling

To Princeton, Sterling

TRAIL LEGEND

Multi-Use Bike Trail

Hiking Trail

Boundary Line

Paved Road

Unpaved Road-Hiking, Mtn. Biking, X-C Skiing allowed.

0   ½   1   2   Miles

Lynn Woods

Grid	D11
Length	40 miles
Surface	Singletrack, doubletrack, fire roads
Setting	Rocky and sandy surfaces, some difficult climbs
Difficulty	Easy to difficult
Acres	2,200
Fees	None
Hours	Sunrise to sunset
Vicinity	Lynn
Lat/Long	42-28/70-55 Trailhead off Pennybrook Road
County	Essex
Contact	Lynn Woods Park Ranger 781-477-7123 Lynn City Hall 3 City Hall Square Lynn, MA 01901 781-598-4000
Facilities	

Getting There
From Boston, north on US-1 to Route 129

Main (west) Entrance – Exit Route 129 right on Walnut St. to Pennybrook Road, then left to the parking area.

Eastern Entrance – Continue on Route 129 (Lynnwood Street) to Great Woods Road.

Trail Notes

Lynn Woods Reservation is located in Lynn, Massachusetts, and is the second largest municipal park in the United States. Bikers must stay on officially marked trails. These trails are posted with a colored paint blaze. Horseback riding is permitted on orange blazed fire roads only. Mountain biking is not allowed between January 1 and April 15, and on trails marked "foot traffic only". Contact the park ranger for cultural history tours, such as Dungeon Rock. The Rose Garden and Wolf Pits are open to the public year round. Picnic area are located near the main entrance, and on Great Woods Road, 1.3 mails from the east entrance and 1.7 miles from the main entrance.

The entire reservation is surrounded by gravel fire roads and seemingly endless, singletrack routes. Each route is numbered, but you will probably need a map to keep from getting lost. The city's reservoir divides the woods in half. The easier riding is on the wider paths of gravel, but even then it can get somewhat steep. The more difficult area is the ridgeline to the north of Walden Pond. The trails vary from large rocks, hilly climbs, mud sucking swamp, to areas laden with logs and other riding hindrances. A worthwhile destination is Dungeon Rock, which is open from 9 am to 2:30 pm from May 1st to October 31st. You can get there by following the signs to Dungeon Road. There is lots of technical singletrack in the hills around Walden Pond. Bowridge is also suggested as a good area for more technical rock climbs and descents. The trail up Wolf Pits will confront you with some huge boulders and tricky ledges.

Official Trail Markings

Fire Roads	=	orange
Nature Trails	=	green
Overlook Trail	=	red
All Other Trails	=	blue

Please stay on official trails and roads

TRAIL LEGEND	
———————	Multi-Use Bike Trail
———————	Paved Road
-----------	Unpaved Road
———————	Road/Highway
·–·–·–·–·–	Power/Pipe Line
– – – – –	Boundary Line

Lynn Woods (continued)

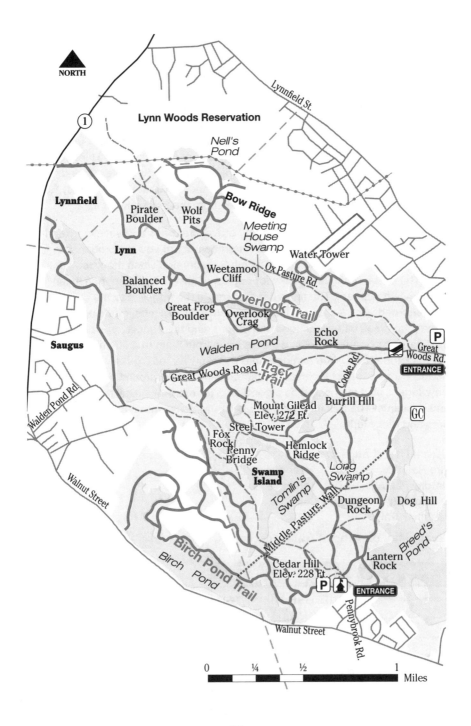

Manuel F. Correllus State Forest

Grid	MV
Length	22 miles
Surface	Paved, doubletrack. singletrack
Setting	Woods, scrubland, fire lanes
Difficulty	Easy
Acres	5,343
Hours	Dawn to dusk
Vicinity	Edgartown
Lat/Long	41-24/70-36 Trailhead area
County	Dukes
Contact	Manuel F. Correllus State Forest Martha's Vineyard 508-693-2540
Facilities	P

Getting There

Martha's Vineyard is located about 7-miles off the southeast coast of Massachusetts, and is about 20 miles long and 10 miles wide. The 5,143-acre forest is located in the heart of the island. You might want to consider leaving your car at one of the parking areas maintained by the ferry companies to avoid the need for ferry reservations and finding parking on the island. From Edgartown, take Edgartown-Vineyard Haven Road for about 5-miles to Sanderson Avenue. Left for a mile to the trailhead behind the fire road barrier gate. You can also buy bus passes at the Edgartown Visitors Center to connect with the towns of Oak Bluffs, Vineyard Haven, Aquinnah, Chilmark, and West Tisbury. The buses are equipped with bike racks.

Manuel F. Correllus State Forest (continued)

Trail Notes

The Forest has 14 miles of paved trail and 7 miles of designated multi-use trails consisting of dirt fire roads, doubletrack, and singletrack. These trails, plus the many miles of other trails that crisscross the forest that are so extensive that you might not see anyone else for most of your ride. The trails are relatively flat with small, gentle rolling hills making for an easy cruise. The forest supports an abundance of woodlands and scrublands, dominated by mixed oak-pine.

Biking around Martha's Vineyard:

The "down-Island" route – takes you from Vineyard Haven to Oak Bluffs to Edgartown and back, for roughly a 25-mile round trip. This route is mostly flat and easy.

The "up-Island" route – runs between Chilmark and Aquinnah. The terrain can be hilly and the roadway curvy. Also there are no bike paths or streetlights. .

If you have the inclination to head for a beach, here are some suggestions from which to choose:

Fuller Street Beach – located at the end of Fuller Street near Lighthouse Beach in Edgartown.

Joseph Sylvia State Beach – two miles long and located along Beach Road between Oak Bluffs and Edgartown. There are lifeguards in season.

Lighthouse Beach – located at Starbuck's Neck, off North Water Street near the center of Edgartown.

Norton Point – this is a three-mile long barrier beach located at the end of Katama Road on the south shore of Edgartown.

South Beach State Park – contains a mile long beach between Herring Creek Road and Katama Road. Expect rough surf, but there are lifeguards in season.

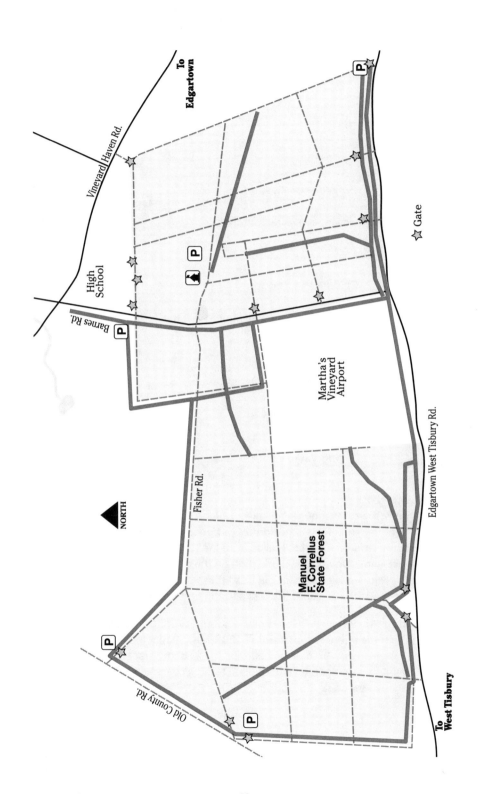

NORTH

To
Edgartown

Vineyard Haven Rd.

High
School

Barnes Rd.

Gate

Martha's
Vineyard
Airport

Edgartown West Tisbury Rd.

Fisher Rd.

Manuel
F. Correllus
State Forest

Old County Rd.

To
West Tisbury

Marblehead Rail Trail

Grid	D11
Length	5 miles
Surface	Gravel, asphalt, sand
Setting	Urban, converted rail-trail
Difficulty	Easy
Vicinity	Marblehead, Salem
Lat/Long	42-30/70-52 Pleasant Street trailhead
County	Essex
Contact	Marblehead Chamber of Commerce 62 Pleasant Street Marblehead, MA 01945 781-631-2868
Facilities	

Getting There

To start from Tower School: Take Route 128 to Route 114 (Exit 25A) and head south to Marblehead. Note that Route 114 becomes Lafayette Street and then Pleasant Street. About 5.3 miles from the Route 128 exit ramp, take a left on West Shore Drive. Down this road on the right is Tower School. Just past the entrance, next to where the trail crosses is a parking area on your right. Cross over the street to the trail and the Letterbox.

To start from Roundhouse Road: Follow Route 114 for 6-miles into Marblehead through the intersection of Route 129 where it becomes Pleasant Street. Continue on Pleasant Street for a half-mile to Bessom Street and turn left to a parking lot on your right at Roundhouse Road. The trail starts across the street at the yellow cable.

Trail Notes

The Marblehead Rail Trail is located north of Boston, passing through the seaside communities of Marblehead, Salem and Swampscott. It follows the old railbed of the Swampscott Branch of the Eastern Railroad, and is approximately 9-feet wide. Parking is available at Bessom Street in Marblehead and along Lafayette Street in Salem. The trail has two connected spurs: one from Lafayette Street in Salem to Bessom Street in Marblehead, and the other from Bessom Street to Seaview Avenue in Swampscott. It also connects with the new, half-mile Salem Bike Trail, which is asphalt paved to Canal Street.

A suggested starting point is from the intersection of Bessom Street and Roundhouse Road in Marblehead. You begin on a sandy path for a quarter mile to the trail junction by a fenced utility yard. The left branch takes you down the coast toward Swampscott, while the right takes you towards Salem. The Swampscott branch of the trail begins on sand and gravel, and then continues on asphalt once past the public high school. The branch towards Salem begins on a sandy surface, passing through the Hawthorn Pond and Wyman Woods Conservation areas. After entering Salem, the trail crosses Route 114, past artistic gates imaged after high-wheel bicycles where it continues with an asphalt surface.

While you are in the area, why not take a ride around Marblehead Neck, if you don't mind road biking. From Pleasant Street, take Ocean Avenue across a causeway past a view of Marblehead Harbor with its 1,600 moored boats. A road loops around the Neck, providing scenic stops at Castle Rock and Chandler Hovey Park and its lighthouse, and Massachusetts Bay.

Marblehead Rail Trail (continued)

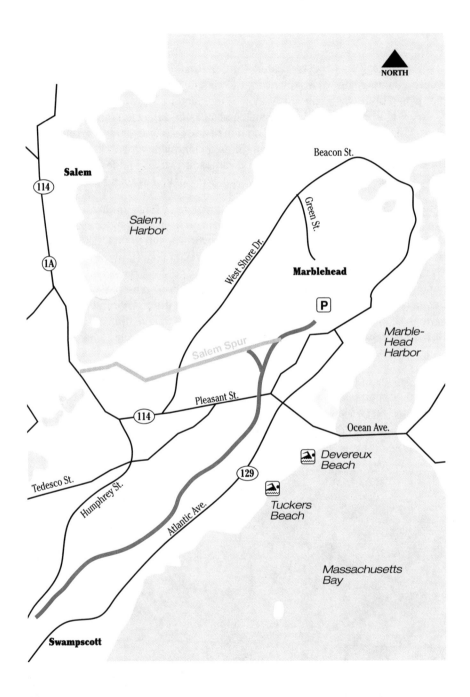

Massasoit State Park

Grid	F11
Length	20 miles
Surface	Singletrack, doubletrack
Setting	Heavily wooded, rolling and short steep hills, roots & rocks
Difficulty	Easy to difficult
Acres	1,500
Hours	Dawn to dusk
Vicinity	Middleboraugh
Lat/Long	41-53/70-60 Trailhead off Massasoit Park Road
County	Bristol
Contact	Massasoit State Park Middleboro Avenue East Taunton 508-822-7405
Facilities	

Getting There
From Boston – Take Route 24 south to Route 44, and then east. At the first traffic light, turn right onto South Street. At the end of the street turn left onto Middleboro Avenue and continue for about 2 miles to the park entrance on the right.

From Worester – take Route 495 to Route 18 (Exit 5) in Middleborough. Go south to Taunton Street, which is the first intersection. Turn right on Taunton Street (it becomes Middleboro Avenue). Go 2.5 miles to the park entrance on the left.

Massasoit State Park (continued)

From Fall River or Providence – Take Route 195 East to Route 24 North. At Route 44 go east to the first traffic light. Turn right onto South Street and follow it to the end. Turn left onto Middleboro Avenue and continue for about 2 miles to the park entrance on the right.

Trail Notes

The park is located just a couple of miles from I-495 in Taunton, Massachusetts. This is a heavily wooded park offering beautiful scenery and many recreation opportunities. Besides biking, there is hiking, horseback riding, cross-country skiing, picnicking, canoeing, camping, and a swimming beach at Middle Pond. The campground provides restrooms, water and electric hookups, but no showers. Bikers generally use the parking lot near the main entrance off Middleborough Avenue. Equestrians mainly use the parking area in the northern part of the forest.

Most of the trails are rolling singletrack, ranging between easy and moderate. There are some short, but steep downhills. The surface is sandy and gravely, with occasional roots and rocks. Heading southwest from the trailhead just behind the main parking area, you come to a fork that takes you either northward or southward on a network of trails. Above Blackhole Pond, in the southeastern part of the park is another network of trails. These trails hook up with a trail paralleling the paved road heading back toward the parking area.

TRAIL LEGEND	
···········	Biking & Hiking Trail
▪▪▪▪▪▪▪▪▪	Biking & Equestrian Trail
————	Paved Road
▪ ▪ ▪ ▪ ▪ ▪	Unpaved Road
▬▬▬▬▬	Road/Highway
– – – – –	Boundary Line

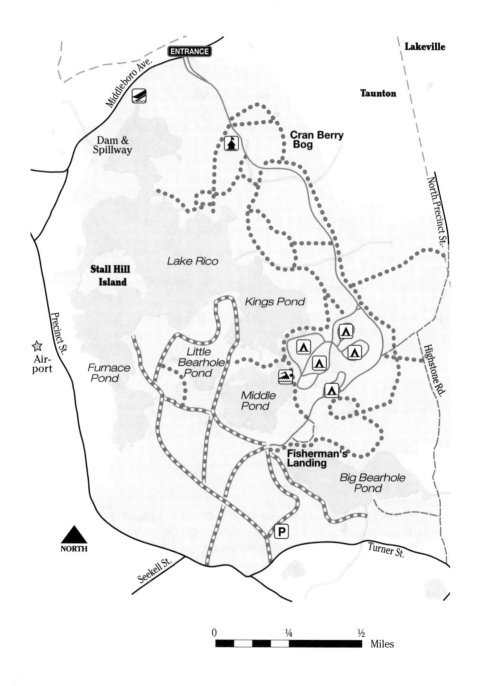

Lakeville

Taunton

ENTRANCE

Middleboro Ave.

Dam &
Spillway

Cran Berry
Bog

North Precinct St.

Lake Rico

Stall Hill
Island

Kings Pond

Precinct St.

☆
Air-
port

Furnace
Pond

Little
Bearhole
Pond

Middle
Pond

Highstone Rd.

Fisherman's
Landing

Big Bearhole
Pond

P

Turner St.

▲
NORTH

Seekell St.

0   ¼   ½
■■■■■■■■■■ Miles

Maudslay State Park

Grid	B11
Length	10 miles
Surface	Doubletrack, some singletrack
Setting	Rolling meadows, grass fields, pine woods
Difficulty	Easy
Acres	480
Fees	Parking fee
Hours	Dawn to dusk
Vicinity	Newburyport
Lat/Long	42-50/70-56 Entrance off Pine Road
County	Essex
Contact	Maudslay State Park Curzon Mill Road Newburyport, MA 978-465-7223
Facilities	P ⛹ ⛱ 🚰

Getting There

From the North or South – Take Route 95 to Route 113 (Exit 57) and follow Route 113 east for a half mile to Noble Street. Go left on Noble Street and then left at the stop sign (Ferry Road). Bear left at the fork and follow the signs.

From the West – Take I-495 to Route 110 (Exit 55) and go east for a mile to Merrill Street. Turn right at the second light. Continue on Merrill (Spofford) Street for 1.5 miles. Take a right before the stop sign onto Ferry Road and follow the signs. There is a small parking fee.

Trail Notes

Situated on the Merrimack River, this former Moseley family estate features rolling meadows, towering pines, 19th century gardens, and one of the largest stands of mountain laurel in Massachusetts. Of special interest are the ornamental trees and masses of azaleas and rhododendrons that bloom in May and June. The trails are open to biking, hiking, horseback riding, and cross-country skiing. Maudslay is host to many outdoor concerts and performances during the summer season. Toward the back of the park, between the field and the Merrimack River is a eagle nesting area. Check with the park ranger for sightings and locations if you to view these birds during their annual visit. Maps are available at the parking lot or Park Headquarters.

The trails are mostly wide, dirt doubletrack, and level except for rolling stretches. They are mowed and generally well maintained. Expect to experience exposed roots. There are also a few singletrack. Some of the trails are layered with mulch and wood chips to minimize rutting from standing water. One trail, about 2 miles long, runs along the Merrimack River, while most of the other trails weave through pine woods, meadows, and across stone bridges.

TRAIL LEGEND	
▬▬▬▬▬	Multi-Use Bike Trail
▬▬▬▬▬	Merrimack River Trail - Multi-Use
∙∙∙∙∙∙∙∙∙	Merrimack River Trail - Hiking
●●●●●●●●●	Hiking/Ski Trail
▪▪▪▪▪▪▪▪	Equestrian Trail
▬▬▬▬▬	Paved Road
▬ ▬ ▬ ▬	Unpaved Road
▬▬▬▬▬	Road/Highway

Maudslay State Park (continued)

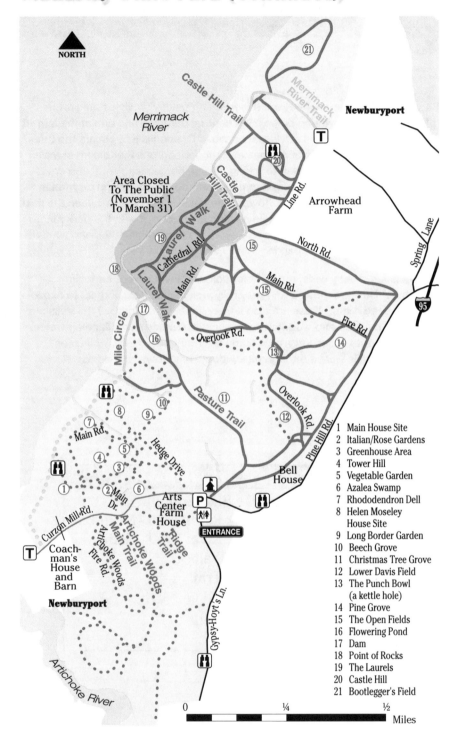

1 Main House Site
2 Italian/Rose Gardens
3 Greenhouse Area
4 Tower Hill
5 Vegetable Garden
6 Azalea Swamp
7 Rhododendron Dell
8 Helen Moseley
   House Site
9 Long Border Garden
10 Beech Grove
11 Christmas Tree Grove
12 Lower Davis Field
13 The Punch Bowl
   (a kettle hole)
14 Pine Grove
15 The Open Fields
16 Flowering Pond
17 Dam
18 Point of Rocks
19 The Laurels
20 Castle Hill
21 Bootlegger's Field

Minuteman Bikeway
Bedford Narrow-Gauge Rail Trail
Reformatory Branch Trail
Battle Road Trail

Minuteman Bikeway

Grid	D10
Length	11 miles
Surface	Asphalt
Setting	Suburban, former railroad line
Difficulty	Easy
Hours	5 am to 9 pm
Vicinity	Arlington, Bedford, Cambridge, Lexington
Lat/Long	42-25/71-09 East Arlington trailhead at Spy Pond Field
County	Middlesex
Contact	Arlington Bicycle Advisory Committee 730 Massachusetts Avenue Arlington, MA 02476 781-316-3090 Arlington Town Hall Planning Dept. 730 Massachusetts Avenue Arlington, MA 02476 781-316-3000
Facilities	

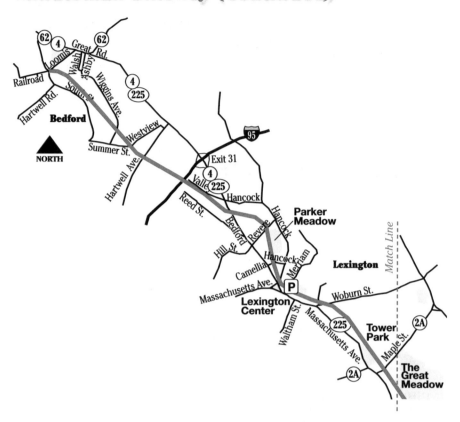

Getting There

Bedford trailhead – Take I-95 to Route 4/225 (Exit 31B) and head north for 1.1 miles. Take a left onto Loomis Street. The trailhead is along side the Bedford Depot Park at the South Road intersection.

Cambridge trailhead – Take I-95 to the Concord Turnpike/Route 2 (Exit 29A), and head east. At the end of the turnpike, bear east onto Alewife Brook Parkway. Take a right at Cambridge Park Drive to the station. West of the station is the trailhead and parking.

East Arlington trailhead - The Alewife Transit Station near the juncture of Routes 2 and 16.

Bicycles are allowed on MBTA Commuter Rail and subway trains (Red, Orange, and Blue Line) all day on weekends and during off-peak hours on weekdays (Mon-Fri: 10am-2pm and after & 7:30pm). You don't need a special pass to bring your bike. The Alewife "T" Station, at the east end of the Minuteman Bikeway, provides access to & from the metro-Boston subway system via the Red Line. There are also numerous bike routes. For information call 800-392-6100.

Trail Notes

This popular trail passes through the historic area where the American Revolution began in 1775. Opened in 1992, the Minuteman Bikeway is built on roadbed of the Lexington & West Cambridge Railroad. The trail is asphalt paved, and 12 feet wide. There are mile marker posts. Refreshments and toilets are available at Depot Park in Bedford, Lexington Visitor's Center, Alewife Station, and nearby businesses.

Heading northwest from Cambridge, the bikeway connects Arlington, Lexington, and Bedford, providing easy access to the Spy Pond and Great Meadows natural areas, as well as neighborhoods and schools. At 1.5 miles into your ride, you'll come to Swan Place in Arlington. Take a short road or sidewalk jog to the right and proceed to Massachusetts Avenue. Turn right toward the Cyrus E. Dallin Art Museum on the right and look for the continuance of the bikeway across Mystic Street. The Lexington Visitor Center, not too much further, is a good place to stop for information on local attractions. Proceeding north you'll pass through a quiet wooded corridor before reaching the end of the trail at Bedford Depot Park. From there you can continue west on the Reformatory Branch Trail or north on the Bedford Narrow-Gauge Trail.

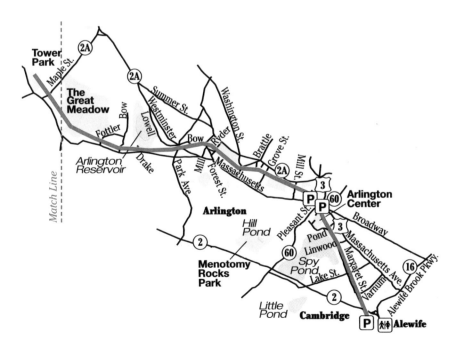

Bedford Narrow-Gauge Rail-Trail

Grid	D10
Length	3 miles
Surface	Asphalt, crushed stone dirt
Setting	Woods, residences
Difficulty	Easy
Vicinity	Bedford
Lat/Long	42-29/71-17 Bedford Depot Park trailhead
County	Middlesex
Contact	Friends of Bedford Depot Park 781-687-6180 www.bedforddepot.org
Facilities	

Getting There
Bedford Park trailhead: Take I-95 to State Route 4/225 (Exit 31B) north toward Bedford for 1.1 miles to Route 225. Take a left on Loomis Street (becomes Railroad Avenue) to the trailhead parking area.

Trail Notes
This trail extends north from Depot Park in Bedford, past woods and residences to the Billerica town line. It follows the Billerica & Bedford Railroad railbed, the nation's first 2-foot narrow gauge railway. The trail surface is a combination of asphalt, crushed stone and dirt. The trail begins at Loomis Street, by a set of metal gates. The ride takes you by the memorial Park gardens, a retail district, and the York Conservation Area. The trail ends at another set of metal gates at the Billerica town line. You can stop for refreshments and information at the old Fright House at the Minuteman Bikeway terminus. It's open on weekends between 10am and 6pm during the bikeway season.

Reformatory Branch Trail

Grid	D10
Length	4.5 miles
Surface	Unimproved
Setting	Natural areas, urban
Difficulty	Easy
Vicinity	Bedford, Concord
Lat/Long	42-29/71-17 Bedford Depot Park trailhead
County	Middlesex
Contact	Friends of Bedford Depot Park
	120 South Road
	Bedford, MA 01730
	781-687-6180
	www.bedforddepot.org
Facilities	P 🚻 ⛲ ♿

Getting There

Bedford Park trailhead: Take I-95 to State Route 4/225 (Exit 31B) north toward Bedford for 1.1 miles to Route 225. Take a left on Loomis Street (becomes Railroad Avenue) to the trailhead parking area.

Trail Notes

The Reformatory Branch Trail takes you westbound from the Bedford Depot Park trailhead on Railroad Avenue. The ride will take you through the Elm Brook Conservation Area, the Mary Putnam Webber Wildlife Preserve, and the Great Meadows National Wildlife Refuge. At the Concord Turnpike, you'll have to cross a gravel parking lot and continue across the street behind the guardrail. Once past this narrow path, there is a small hill to descend before returning to the main trail. As you get closer to Concord there are several roads to cross. The trail ends after crossing Lowell Road at the Concord River.

Battle Road Trail

Grid	D10
Length	5.5 miles
Surface	Gravel, hard pack dirt
Setting	Farm fields, parkland
Difficulty	Easy
Hours	Dawn to dusk
Vicinity	Concord, Lexington
Lat/Long	42-27/71-16 Minute Man National Historic Park
County	Middlesex
Contact	Minute Man National Historic Park 978-369-6993
Facilities	

Getting There

Minute Man Visitor Center near Lexington: From take I-95 to Route 2A West (Exit 30B). Signs for the Visitor's Center and parking will be seen a short distance further. From Concord: Go left on Monument Street and follow the signs. Continue past Orchard House and Wayside to the parking area.

Trail Notes

The Battle Road Trail is a 5.5-mile pathway in Lexington, Lincoln, and Concord that marks the path once trodden by British soldiers on their way from Boston to Concord, where they had marched to seize a supply of arms the colonists had stored. This is primarily an educational trail. Part of the Minute Man National Historic Park, the trail follows Route 2A and runs from Meriam Corner in Concord to Fiske Hill in Lexington. East from Meriam's Corner are the historic farming fields that have remained in the same configuration since the 17th century. From the Brooks parking area you pass a stretch of historic Brooks houses, then a boardwalk through protected wetland, following the route of the Minute Men up a hill, along a stone wall, to the Bloody Angle. West of the Minute Man Visitor Center is the "Minute Man Boulder" and Nelson archeological sites.

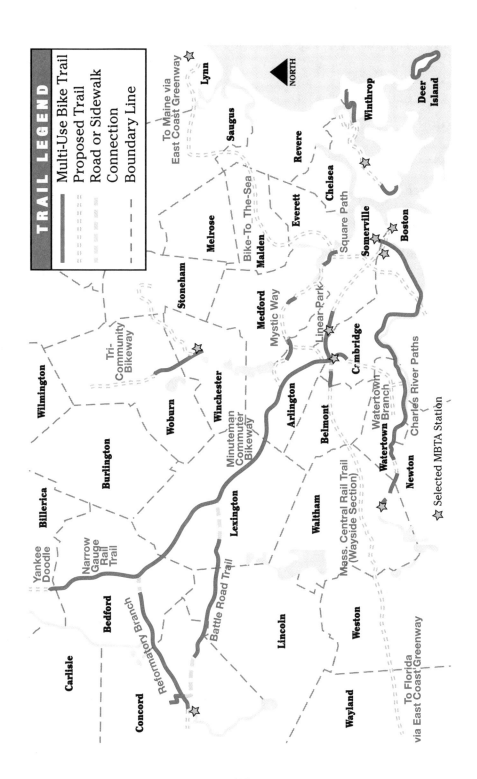

TRAIL LEGEND

	Multi-Use Bike Trail
	Proposed Trail
	Road or Sidewalk Connection
	Boundary Line

NORTH

To Maine via East Coast Greenway

Lynn

Saugus

Revere

Chelsea

Winthrop

Deer Island

Melrose

Everett

Boston

Square Path

Bike-To-The-Sea

Malden

Somerville

Stoneham

Medford

Mystic Way

Linear Park

Tri-Community Bikeway

Winchester

Cambridge

Wilmington

Woburn

Arlington

Watertown

Burlington

Minuteman Commuter Bikeway

Belmont

Watertown Branch

Charles River Paths

Billerica

Lexington

Waltham

Newton

Yankee Doodle

Narrow Gauge Rail Trail

Battle Road Trail

Mass. Central Rail Trail (Wayside Section)

Bedford

Lincoln

Weston

Selected MBTA Station

Carlisle

Reformatory Branch

Concord

Wayland

To Florida via East Coast Greenway

Mount Greylock State Reservation

Grid	C2
Length	20 miles
Surface	Old fire roads, singletrack
Setting	Abandoned farmland, woodland
Difficulty	Easy to difficult
Acres	12,500
Hours	Sunrise to a half hour after sunset
Vicinity	Adams, New Ashford
Lat/Long	42-36/73-12 Trailhead off Rockwell Road
County	Berkshire
Contact	Mount Greylock State Reservation Rockwell Road Lanesborough, MA 01237 413-499-4263
Facilities	P 舟 禾 🏠 🍴 🅰 ♿

Getting There
From the south, take I-90 to Route 20 west (Exit 2) in Lee for 11.8 miles to Route 7 in Pittsfield. Go north on Route 7 for 6.6 miles to Lanesborough. At the Mount Greylock sign turn right onto North Main Street. Follow the brown sign 1.5 miles from route 76 to the Visitors Center and trailhead.

From North Adams, take Route 2 west for 1.2 mile to the Mount Greylock Reservation sign on the left.

From Williamstown, take Route 2 east for 3.7 miles, then turn right onto Notch Road. Follow the brown signs for 2.5 miles to the reservation entrance trailhead.

Trail Notes

Mount Greylock is located in the northern Berkshires in the northwest corner of western Massachusetts, 18 miles north of Pittsfield. At 3,491 feet, it is the highest point in the state, and also the oldest state forest in Massachusetts, established in 1898. The reservation remains open to mountain biking, but is closed to auto traffic into the 2009 season. The setting is wild and rugged and yet accessible. Herman Melville was so enthralled with the mountain that he set up a special observation deck at his home at Arrowhead by Pittsfield. The Visitors Center, on the Lanesborough side of the mountain, off Route 7 and Rockwell Road, is open daily from Memorial Day through Labor Day from 9 am to 10 pm, and from 9 am to 4 pm the remainder of the year. The Center provides exhibits and information on the park and surrounding area. There is primitive overnight camping on Sperry Road. It has composting toilets, but no potable water. The 92-foot high War Veteran's Memorial Tower, built in 1932, is open daily during the summer and fall and offers views up to 100 miles.

Mount Greylock offers over 70 miles of designated trails, including 20 miles for mountain biking, and an 11.5-mile section of the Appalachian National Scenic Trail. A convenient starting point is from the Jones Nose parking area. Ride around the gate and downhill on Old Adams Road to a small brook from which you can stay on Old Adams Road by forking left, or to the right on a scenic trial that heads toward the town of Cheshire. Among the riding opportunities is the Stony Ledge Trail that descends from the scenic overlook at the top of Sperry Road. This is an out-and-back ride, often wet and treacherous, that climbs past the camping area. Another is the rugged ride that climbs and descends for several miles through deep woods from a starting point on Rockwell Road to the Cheshire Harbor Trail. The road to the top of the mountain is closed, but you can still hike up there. The 11.2-mile Ashuwillticook Rail-Trail is also located nearby, between Mount Greylock and the Hoosac Mountains.

TRAIL LEGEND	
━━━━━━	Multi-Use Bike Trail
≡≡≡≡≡≡≡	Ashuwillticook Rail Trail
▬ ▬ ▬ ▬ ▬	Appalachian Trail
••••••••••	Trail
━━━━━━	Paved Road
▬▬▬▬▬▬	Unpaved Road
– – – – –	Boundary Line

Mount Greylock State Reservation
(continued)

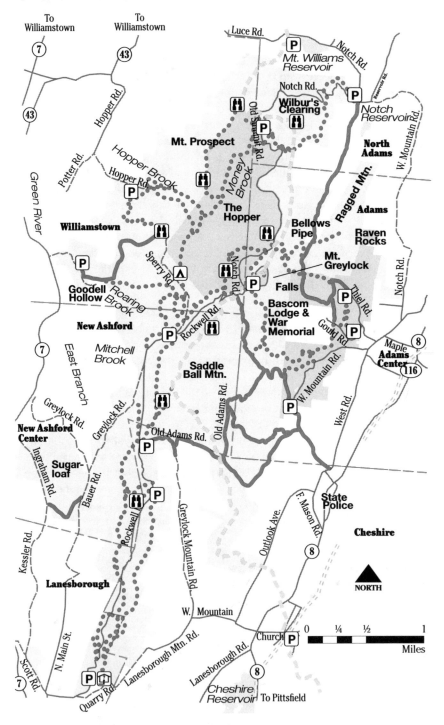

Courtesy of the Massachusetts Department of Conservation & Recreation. Photo by Kindra Clineff for the DCR©

Myles Standish State Forest

Grid	F12
Length & Surface	16 miles paved 30 miles of unpaved roads, grass & loose sand
Setting	Deep forest, mainly flat with short climbs, ponds
Difficulty	Easy to moderate
Acres	14,651
Hours	Dawn to dusk
Vicinity	Plymouth, Carver
Lat/Long	41-50/70-42 Entrance off East Head/Cranberry Rd.
County	Plymouth
Contact	Myles Standish State Forest Cranberry Road South Carver, MA 02366 508-866-2526
Facilities	P ♦♦ ⊼ ▲

Getting There

From the North: Take Route 3 south to Long Pond Road west (Exit 5) and continue for about 3 miles to the forest entrance on the right. There is parking at Forest Headquarters.

From the Southeast: Take Route 3 north to Long Pond Road (Exit 2), and then right for 2 miles to the forest entrance.

From I-495: Take I-495 to its intersection with Route 58 (Exit 2) at South Carver and go north to Cranberry Road. Follow the signs to the park entrance.

Trail Notes

Myles Standish State Forest sprawls across the southern sections of Plymouth and Carver in southeastern Massachusetts. There are five camping areas, 16 maintained ponds, and a swimming beach. Other activities include picnicking and canoeing. Campground office hours are from 8 am to 8 pm. The Interpretive Center is open from July 1 to the end of September. Off-road vehicles are not allowed in the forest. This area of southern Massachusetts produces more cranberries than any other region in the world.

This is a multi-seasonal mountain biking destination, consisting of sandy doubletrack and singletrack. Mountain biking is allowed anywhere in the forest except the sensitive pond shores and a designated hiking trail near park headquarters. The 35 miles of equestrian trails are recommended for a good ride. They are designated with red markers and are generally less sandy than unpaved roads. There are an almost endless network of trails and forest roads, with many opportunities for both long and short out-and-back loop rides. The unpaved roads vary from hard-packed dirt to grass and loose sand. To avoid getting lost a map, and even a compass is almost a must. Water is only available at forest headquarters or at campsites.

The 16 miles of asphalt paved bike paths has three main sections. One heads along Upper College Pond Road northeast for 5 miles, the second heads along Bare Hill Road northwest for 4 miles, and the third, consisting of several interconnecting loops, goes south for about 7 miles. They extend far into the forest, and provide for exits or short cuts from the off-road sections. These bike paths follow the rolling contours of the land.

Myles Standish State Forest

Courtesy of the Department of Conservation & Recreation. Photo by Kindra Clineff for the DCR©

Myles Standish State Forest (continued)

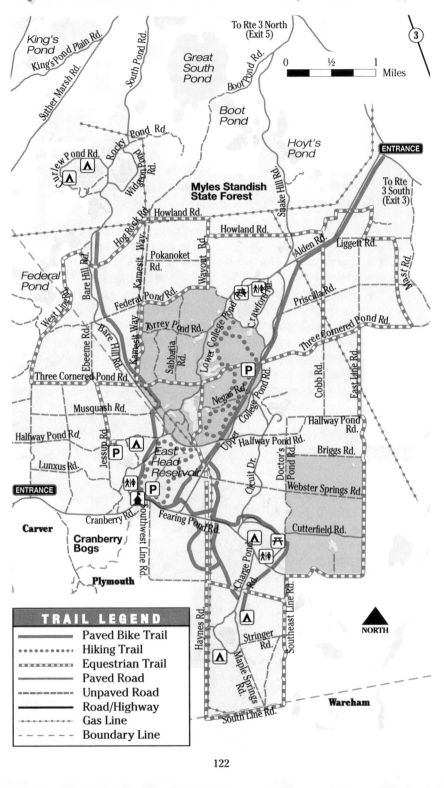

TRAIL LEGEND

————	Paved Bike Trail
··········	Hiking Trail
▪▪▪▪▪▪▪▪▪	Equestrian Trail
————	Paved Road
--------	Unpaved Road
████████	Road/Highway
××××××××	Gas Line
— — — —	Boundary Line

Nashua River Rail Trail

Grid	C8
Length	12.3 miles 11.3 in Massachusetts, 1 mile into Nashua, New Hampshire
Surface	Asphalt
Setting	Suburban, ponds
Difficulty	Easy
Hours	Dawn to dusk
Vicinity	Ayer, Groton, Pepperell, Dunstable
Lat/Long	42-33/71-35 Ayer trailhead
County	Middlesex
Contact	Willow Brook State Forest 978-597-8802
Facilities	P

Getting There

Aver Center: Take Route 2, either east or west, to Route 111 (Exit 38B), and then north to the Ayer rotary. Halfway around the rotary turn onto Route 2A. Turn right after Ayer Center and take the first right onto Groton Street. Trail parking is on the right.

Groton Center: Take I-495, either north or south, to Route 119 (Exit 31), and then west for about 7 miles to Groton Center. Turn left at Station Avenue to on street parking beside the trail.

Groton Sand Hill Road: Take I-495, either north or south, to Route 119 (Exit 31) and then west for about 10 miles to Nod Road. From Nod Road turn right on Sand Hill Road, and follow it to the right after crossing the trail.

Dunstable: Take Route 3 to Route 113 (Exit 35) west. Past Dunstable Center, turn right on Hollis Street to the New Hampshire state line and parking on the left.

Nashua River Rail Trail (continued)

Trail Notes

The paved 12-mile Nashua River Rail Trail is located in northern Massachusetts and southern New Hampshire. It roughly follows the course of the Nashua River from Ayer to about a mile across the New Hampshire state border. The trail was developed from the former Hollis branch of the Boston and Maine Railroad line, and officially opened in 2002. Parking and non-flush toilets are available at the Ayer trailhead. Toilet facilities are also available at a service station 8 miles into the trail north from Ayer. The trailhead is across from the Ayer commuter rail station, which offers service between Boston and Fitchburg. There is also a bicycle shop near the trailhead. At the Nashua trailhead, parking is available at Yudicky Park. There is also parking in Groton, Dunstable and Pepperell Center. Other parking lots are located along the trail. Nearby refreshments can be found in Groton Center and in Pepperell, and there is water in front of the Groton Town Hall close to the trail on Station Avenue.

The trail has a 10-foot wide paved surface for the entire length. There is also a 5-foot parallel trail for equestrian use extending from the New Hampshire state line to Groton. The trail offers numerous scenic overlooks as it travels along a varied landscape, especially during the fall foliage season. As it leaves residential Ayer, it follows a rural, tree-lined corridor. The rail trail passes through wetlands, ponds, swamps, woodlands, and a few farms near the end of the trail. Midway through your journey, the trail skirts the J. Harry Rich State Forest and the Nashua River. Along the way you'll have an opportunity to observe a variety of animals such as beaver and herons.

TRAIL LEGEND	
────────	Multi-Use Bike Trail
▬ ▬ ▬ ▬ ▬	On-Street
▪▪▪▪▪▪▪▪▪▪	Equestrian Trail
────────	Road/Highway
‑ ‑ ‑ ‑ ‑ ‑	Boundary Line

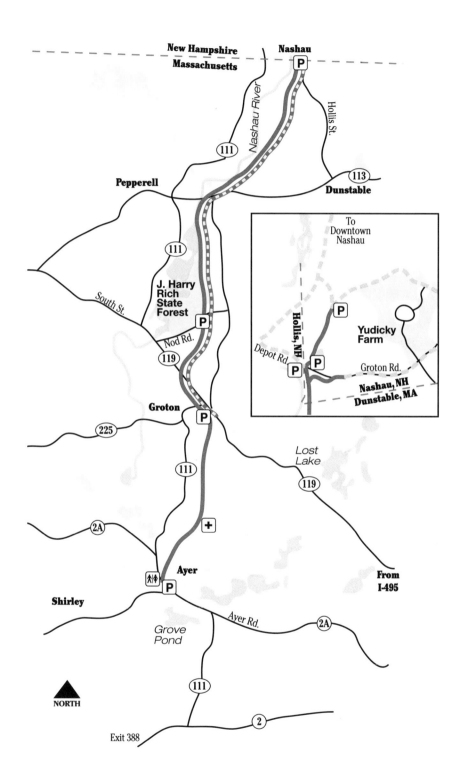

New Hampshire

Massachusetts

Nashau

P

Nashau River

111

Hollis St.

Pepperell

113

Dunstable

111

South St.

J. Harry
Rich
State
Forest

P

Nod Rd.

119

Groton

P

225

111

+

2A

Lost
Lake

119

From
I-495

Ayer

P

Shirley

Grove
Pond

Ayer Rd.

2A

111

2

Exit 388

NORTH

To
Downtown
Nashau

P

Yudicky
Farm

Hollis, NH

Depot Rd.

P

P

Groton Rd.

Nashau, NH
Dunstable, MA

Nickerson State Park

Grid	CC
Length	6 miles paved, 5 miles of fire roads
Surface	Pine needles, soft sand
Setting	Woods, winding, hilly
Difficulty	Easy to moderate
Acres	1,900
Hours	Dawn to dusk
Vicinity	Brewster
Lat/Long	41-47/70-02 Deer Path Road & 6A
County	Barnstable
Contact	Nickerson State Park Route 6A Brewster, MA 508-896-3491
Facilities	

Getting There
From Boston: Take Route 3 south to the Sagamore Bridge, then Route 6 to Exit 12 in Orleans. Turn left off the ramp onto Route 6A West towards Brewster for about 2 miles to the park entrance on the left.

From Route 6, take Route 137 north for 3.8-miles, then east (right) on Route 124 for a half mile. Turn right (eastbound) on Route 6A for 3-miles, then right at the Nickerson State Park entrance. There is a parking area by the contact station.

Trail Notes

Located in Cape Cod, Nickerson State Park is surrounded by woods that slop down to the banks of several crystal clear fresh water ponds. These ponds depend only on groundwater and precipitation causing the water level to fluctuate from season to season and year to year. This is a place to find solitude and wilderness on the Cape during it busy summer season. Facilities include more than 420 campsites with restrooms and showers, yurt camping, picnicking, an amphitheater, swimming beaches, canoeing, and many seasonal interpretive and recreational programs provided by park staff.

The 6-mile paved bike trail is 6 feet wide, and connects to the 25-mile Cape Code Rail Trail. Cape Cod Bay is within cycling distance. The trails are winding and hilly through the pine forest, but are generally short. There are many thorns, so expect a flat if you're not careful. The surface is mostly pine needles and sand, with no rocky sections. A favorite ride is the narrow trail that circles Little Cliff pond.

Nickerson State Park

Courtesy of the Massachusetts Department of Conservation & Recreation. Photo by Kindra Clineff©

Nickerson State Park (continued)

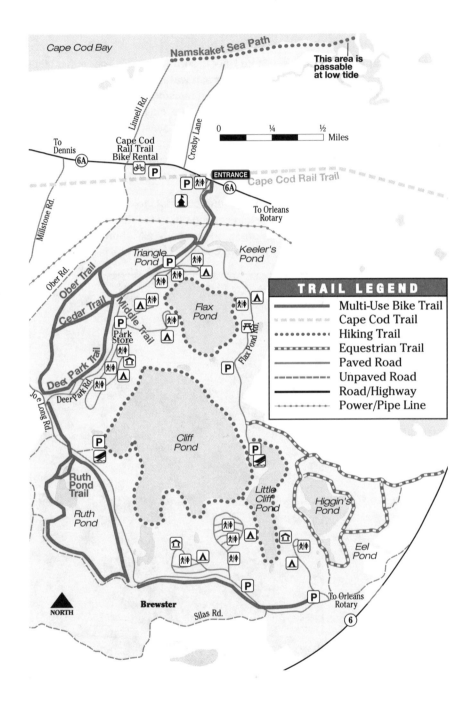

TRAIL LEGEND

———	Multi-Use Bike Trail
– – –	Cape Cod Trail
••••••	Hiking Trail
⌑⌑⌑⌑	Equestrian Trail
———	Paved Road
– – –	Unpaved Road
———	Road/Highway
+•+•+	Power/Pipe Line

Cape Cod Bay

Namskaket Sea Path

This area is passable at low tide

Linnell Rd.

Crosby Lane

0   ¼   ½   Miles

To Dennis

6A

Cape Cod Rail Trail Bike Rental

ENTRANCE

6A

Cape Cod Rail Trail

To Orleans Rotary

Millstone Rd.

Ober Rd.

Ober Trail

Cedar Trail

Middle Trail

Deer Park Trail

Deer Park Rd.

Joe Long Rd.

Triangle Pond

Keeler's Pond

Flax Pond

Park Store

Flax Pond Rd.

Cliff Pond

Little Cliff Pond

Higgin's Pond

Ruth Pond Trail

Ruth Pond

Eel Pond

NORTH

Brewster

Silas Rd.

To Orleans Rotary

6

Norwottuck Rail Trail

Grid	D4
Length	10 miles
Surface	Paved
Setting	Level terrain, urban communities, farms, woods
Difficulty	Easy
Hours	Dawn to dusk, 24/7 for commuters
Vicinity	Amherst, Northampton
Lat/Long	42-20/72-38 Trailhead at Damon Road
County	Hampshire
Contact	Norwottuck Rail Trail 136 Damon Road Northampton, MA 01060 413-586-8706, Ext. 12
Facilities	

Getting There
Take I-90 to Route 91 (Exit 4) and go north to Route 9 (Exit 19). Continue through the traffic lights to Damon Road. There is parking at Elwell State Park on the right. Other parking areas include: both ends of the trail, Route 9 in Hadley behind the Bread and Circus Market at the Mountain Farms Mall, Station Road in Amherst, and the junction of Mill Lane and Southeast Street in Amherst.

Trail Notes
Part of the Connecticut River Greenway State Park, the Norwottuck Rail trail stretches from Elwell State Park, connecting the towns of Northampton, Hadley, and Amherst. You start out by crossing the Connecticut River on a 1492-foot iron bridge, paralleling the Calvin Coolidge Bridge. Approaching Hadley, Mount Holyoke can be seen rising in the distance. The trail paral-

lels Route 9. In Hadley you'll pass its former railroad station and on through Hadley Commons. There is a bicycle rental shop about 3 miles into the ride, and the Route 9 underpass is a little further. Continuing on past Hampshire Mall to the Belchertown trailhead brings you to Route 116, where you can get off the trail and go north for a short distance to Amherst.

Amherst is home to Amherst College and the University of Massachusetts. Just before the downtown area is a connector trail leading to a 2-mile student commuter path known as the UMass bikeway. Back on the rail trail near the end, along an active rail corridor, you will pass over the Mill River and East Street trestle bridges. The final stretch passes wetlands and ponds before reaching the northern trailhead and parking at Warren Wright Road.

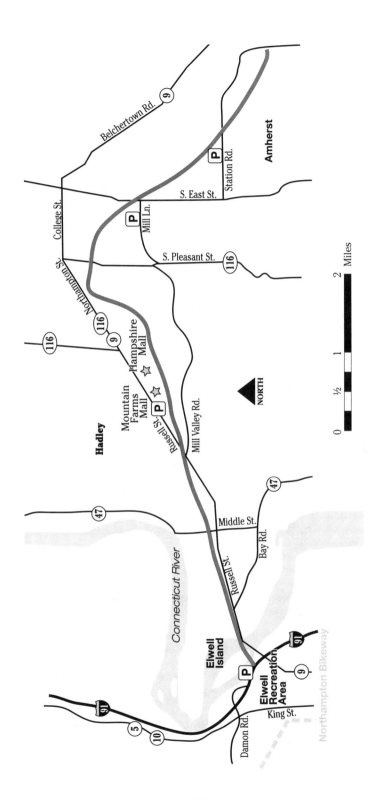

October Mountain State Forest

Grid	D2
Length	30 miles
Surface	Singletrack, rugged jeep roads, smooth dirt roads.
Setting	Deep woods, bushes, lakes, steep hills, lakes
Difficulty	Moderate to difficult
Acres	16,500
Hours	Sunrise to one half-hour after sunset
Vicinity	Pittsfield, Lenox
Lat/Long	42-22/73-09 Pittsfield Road & W Branch Road
County	Berkshire
Contact	October Mountain State Forest 256 Woodland Road Lee, MA 413-243-1778
Facilities	

Getting There
From the East or West: Take I-90 to Route 20 (Exit 2 in Lee). Go west on Route 20 for 1.1 miles through downtown Lee to Center Street. Turn right on Center Street (becomes Columbus Street) for 1 mile to Bradley Street. Take a right on Bradley Street (becomes Woodland Road) and follow the brown signs 1 mile to the campground entrance.

From North of South: Take Route 7 (merges with Route 20) to Lenox. At Walker Street turn west (left from north or right from south) for 2.5 miles to Lenoxdale. Turn right on Mill Street, cross a bridge and continue for 0.5 miles to Bradley Street. Take a left on Bradley Street (becomes Woodland Road) and follow the brown signs for 1 mile to the campground entrance.

Trail Notes

Located in the Berkshires, October Mountain is the largest state forest in Massachusetts. The name is attributed to writer Herman Melville, who was so impressed with the scenic beauty of these hills with his view from his home in Pittsfield during the fall months. Camping season is normally from mid-May through mid-October. Campground office hours are from 8am to 10pm. There are no electric hook-ups. ATV's are permitted during daylight hours only on designated trails. The setting varies from highland pines to snack able berry bushes, several large lakes and a dam.

The trails range from rugged jeep roads, smoother dirt roads, to single-track. One option is to start out at the campground on the western edge of the forest that provides a series of steep changes in elevation between the Housatonic River and the forest's interior. Another route is to take Schermer-horn Road, which rises from the Housatonic River a short distance north of the campground and heads southeast to Becket. There is a "T" intersection at the top of the mountain. Turn right and you will end up on County Road, which runs to Route 8.

Still another option is to proceed north on Woodland Road as you leave the campground. About a mile in, at the Housatonic River, turn to the right past Schernerhorn Road, continue north to New Lenox Road, and then turn right. This paved road soon becomes a climbing dirt road. At the "T" intersec-tion take a right past the Farnum Reservoir and a dirt road (Schermerhorn Road) on the right. Further on you will come to a 4-way intersection with West Branch Road on the top of the mountain. To return to the campground, ride southeast onto County Road westward until it turns sharply to the right. Go left on a rugged road that descends along a stream bed and eventually becomes Washington Mountain Road. At the stop sign, take a right on the paved Woodland Road running past the campground on the right.

TRAIL LEGEND	
───────	Multi-Use Bike Trail
▪ ▬ ▬ ▬ ▬ ▬ ▬	Appalachian Trail
• • • • • • • • • • • ◖	Hiking Trail
───────	Paved Road
▬ ▬ ▬ ▬ ▬ ▬ ▬ ▬	Unpaved Road
━━━━━━━	Road/Highway
───────	Utility Corridor
– – – – – –	Boundary Line

October Mountain State Forest (continued)

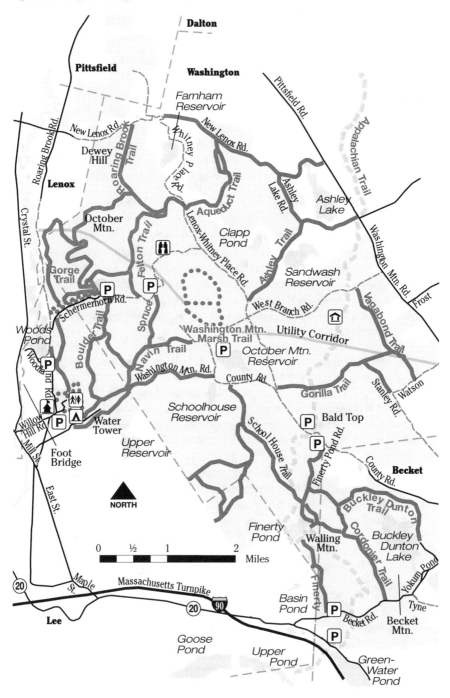

Dalton

Pittsfield

Washington

Farnham Reservoir

New Lenox Rd.

New Lenox Rd.

Roaring Brook Rd.

Whitney Place Rd.

Dewey Hill

Roaring Brook Trail

Pittsfield Rd.

Appalachian Trail

Lenox

Crystal St.

October Mtn.

Aqueduct Trail

Clapp Pond

Ashley Lake Rd.

Ashley Lake

Washington Mtn. Rd.

Felton Trail

Lenox-Whitney Place Rd.

Ashley Trail

Gorge Trail

Sandwash Reservoir

Frost

P

Schermerhorn Rd.

P

Spruce

West Branch Rd.

Vagabond Trail

Woods Pond

Boulder Trail

Washington Mtn. Marsh Trail

Navin Trail

Washington Mtn. Rd.

P

October Mtn. Reservoir

Utility Corridor

Woodland Rd.

County Rd.

Gorilla Trail

Stanley Rd.

Watson

Willow Hill Rd.

P

Mill St.

Water Tower

Schoolhouse Reservoir

School House Trail

P

Bald Top

Finerty Pond Rd.

Foot Bridge

Upper Reservoir

P

County Rd.

Becket

East St.

NORTH

Finerty Pond

Buckley Dunton Trail

Cordonier Trail

Walling Mtn.

Buckley Dunton Lake

0   ½   1   2
Miles

Yokum Pond

Maple St.

Massachusetts Turnpike

Basin Pond

Finerty

Tyne

20

20   90

Becket Rd.

Becket Mtn.

Lee

P

Goose Pond

Upper Pond

Green-Water Pond

Otter River State Forest

Grid	C6
Length	18 miles
Surface	Singletrack, doubletrack, dirt roads
Setting	Woodlands, open areas, mostly flat, some hilly areas
Difficulty	Easy to moderate
Acres	12,788
Fees	$5.00 camping and beach area
Hours	Sunrise to 8pm
Vicinity	Baldenville, Royalston, Winchendon
Lat/Long	42-37/72-05 Trailhead off US202 & Elm
County	Worcester
Contact	Otter River State Forest New Winchendon Road Baldwinville, MA 978-939-8962
Facilities	

Getting There

From the east: Take Route 2 west to Baldwinville Road (Exit 20), then right to the end. Turn right again on Route 202 north for 1.2 miles to the park entrance on the left.

From the west: Take Route 2 east to Route 202 (Exit 19), then north (right) for 4.8 miles to the park entrance on the left.

Otter River State Forest (continued)

Trail Notes

Otter River State Forest is located in north central Massachusetts, near Baldwinville. After the state acquired the land in 1915, it was reforested with groves of pines. Oak and hickory, northern hardwood, and the pines make up the current three forest types. Deer, pheasant, duck, beaver, fox and mink are all common. The forest is also home to numerous wild flowers and shrubs. Facilities include camping, with restrooms and showers, picnic areas, a swimming beach, and a ball field. These facilities are centered by Beaman Pond. To the north is the Lake Dennison Recreation Area. It is also adjacent to the many miles of mountain bike trails in the Birch Hill Wildlife Management Area. Be aware that this is a popular hunting area in season.

Effort level is easy to moderate. The setting is woodlands and open areas. The ride is mostly level with some short hills. The surface is grassy single-track, doubletrack and dirt roads, which are sometimes rough and rutted. Around the vicinity of the reservoir you can find old fieldstone walls and overgrown apple trees from former pastures and orchards now filled with forest stands. Suggested rides include the 5-mile River Road Loop, the 3-mile Wetmore loop that connects to New Boston Road and links you back with Goodnow Road, and the 1.5-mile Royalston Road Loop.

TRAIL LEGEND	
▬▬▬▬▬	Multi-Use Bike Trail
▬▬▬▬▬	Paved Road
▬ ▬ ▬ ▬	Unpaved Road
▬▬▬▬▬	Road/Highway
++++++++++	Railroad Tracks
– – – – –	Boundary Line

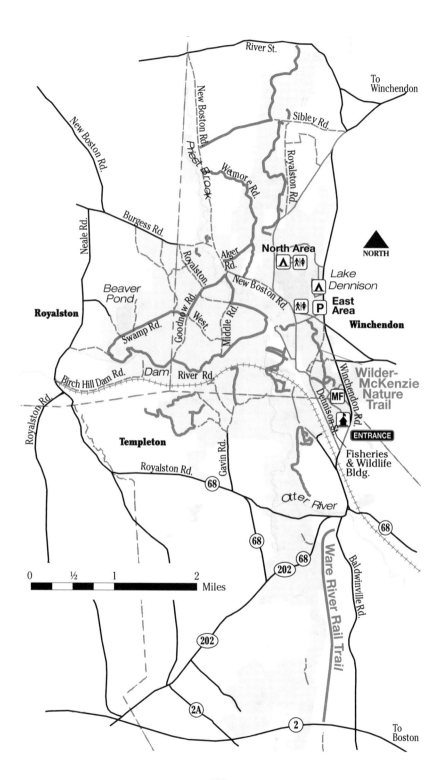

River St.

To
Winchendon

New Boston Rd.

Sibley Rd.

New Boston Rd.

Priest Brook

Wetmore Rd.

Royalston Rd.

Neale Rd.

Burgess Rd.

Royalston Rd.

Alger
Rd.

North Area

NORTH

Lake
Dennison

Beaver
Pond

New Boston Rd.

East
Area

P

Royalston

Goodnow Rd.

West.

Middle Rd.

Winchendon

Swamp Rd.

Royalston Rd.

Birch Hill Dam Rd.

Dam

River Rd.

Winchendon Rd.

MF

Wilder-
McKenzie
Nature
Trail

Dennison St.

ENTRANCE

Templeton

Gavin Rd.

Fisheries
& Wildlife
Bldg.

Royalston Rd.

68

Otter River

68

202

68

68

0   ½   1   2
Miles

Ware River Rail Trail

Baldwinville Rd.

202

2A

202

2

To
Boston

Pittsfield State Forest

Grid	D1
Length	30 miles
Surface	Doubletrack, singletrack
Setting	Deep woods, flat areas to long steep rides
Difficulty	Easy to difficult
Acres	10,000
Fees	$5 vehicle day use between early May to mid-October
Hours	Sunrise to 8pm
Vicinity	Pittsfield
Lat/Long	42-29/73-18 Trailhead off Cascade Street
County	Berkshire
Contact	Pittsfield State Forest 1041 Cascade Street Pittsfield, MA 01201 413-442-8992
Facilities	

Getting There

From the east or west: Take I-90 to Route 210 (Exit 2 in Lee). Go west for 11 miles to Route 20 in downtown Pittsfield. Turn left and continue for 2.2 miles to Hungerford Avenue. Turn right for 0.2 miles, and then bear left onto Fort Hill Avenue for 1 mile. Take a left onto West Street for 0.2 miles, and turn right onto Churchill Street for 1.7 miles to Cascade Street. Turn left and follow the brown signs to the park.

From the north or south: Take Route 7 to Route 20 West. Turn right on Hungerford Avenue for 0.2 miles, and then bear left onto Fort Hill Avenue

for another mile. Turn left onto West Street of 0.2 miles and then turn right onto Churchill Street for 1.7 miles to Cascade Street. Turn left and follow the brown signs to the park.

Trail Notes

Pittsfield State Forest is located in the central Berkshires, in western Massachusetts. The forest follows the crest of the Taconic Mountain Range separating Massachusetts and New York. The vista from the top of Berry Mountain provides a striking panorama and a great place to watch the setting sun. Access is available at several locations to the 35 miles long Taconic Crest Hiking Trail. There are acres of wild azalea fields that generate a profusion of pink blossoms in June. Berry Pond is one of the highest natural water bodies in the state at 2,150 feet in elevation. The forest has two camping areas, two picnic areas, a rustic ski lodge, and a swimming beach. Brook campground, at the mountain's base, has flush toilets. Non-motorized boating is allowed. ATV parking is limited to Balance Rock, and their use on the trails is limited.

There are some 30 miles of trails in which to escape into the quiet and peace of the forest. The easier and shorter loops are either east or west of the park entrance. The more challenging rides are north and south from the top of the ridge near Berry Pond. To get to the ridge from the forest entrance, take the moderately steep Honwee Trail toward the ridge top, and then continue on the paved road for the rest of the way to the top.   The Honwee Trail has two legs. Stay on the one closest to the paved road, as the one that is further is very steep. The loop north follows the Taconic Skyline Trail to Potter Mountain Road, which descends to the left. At the bottom you can visit Balance rock by turning left. To continue your ride, follow Balance Rock Trail back to the bottom of Honwee Trail. To take the route south from Berry Pond descend to West Street, then pick up the CCC Trail to go further south.

TRAIL LEGEND	
———	Multi-Use Bike Trail (non-motorized)
– – – – –	Multi-Use Bike Trail (motorized)
••••••••••	Hiking Trail
———	Paved Road
- - - - - - -	Unpaved Road
━━━━	Road/Highway
– – – – –	Boundary Line

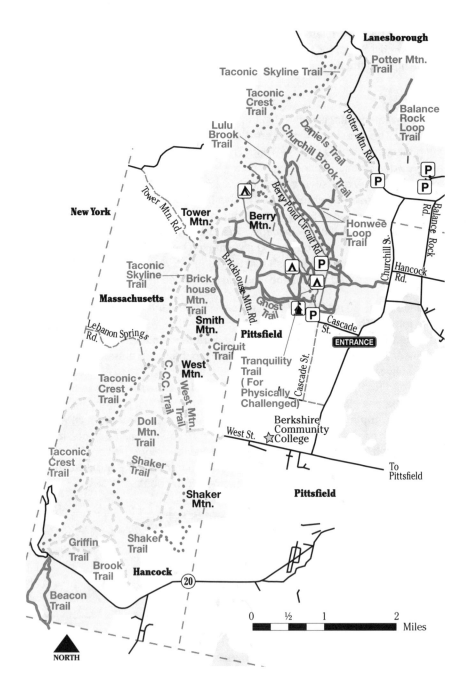

Pittsfield State Forest

Courtesy of the Massachusetts Department of Conservation and Recreation. Photo by Kindra Clineff for the DCR©

Plum Island

Grid	B11
Length	6.5 miles (13 miles round trip)
Surface	Paved & gravel roads
Setting	Sandy, thickets
Difficulty	Easy to moderate
Fees	$2 walking & bicycling, $5 per person by car
Hours	Dawn to dusk
Vicinity	Newbury, Newburyport
Lat/Long	42-49/70-52 Trailhead at Water & Green Street
County	Essex
Contact	Parker River National Wildlife Refuge 6 Plum Island Turnpike Newburyport, MA 01950 978-465-5753
Facilities	

Getting There
Plum Island is accessed by one road running from Newburyport to the north of the island on a causeway and drawbridge over the Plum Island River. From I-1, take a left onto Water Street. Just past Green Street is a parking area and trailhead on your left.

Trail Notes
Plum Island is an 11-mile long barrier beach that extends south of Newburyport. Parker River Wildlife Refuge occupies the southern two-thirds of the island. The island is separated from the mainland by the Parker River. Biking is said to be the best mode of transportation to enjoy the Refuge. Virtually the entire oceanfront is public beach, although much of it is accessible

only by foot. There are boardwalks in the Refuge that take you through the dunes and out onto the beach. The roads are a combination of pavement and gravel, giving you access to 7 miles of this secluded, dune-backed barrier beach. At the northern end of the road is the historic Plum Island Lighthouse. The Visitor's Center is open from 8am to 4:30pm.

Plum Island is a popular vacation destination. You'll find numerous lodging options, including B&B's, inns, and rental cottages. The Plum Island Beach is a gently sloping shelf extending some distance out to sea. Breakers are small and close to shore. The shelf causes strong undertow currents that can draw the unsuspecting swimmer out to sea. During severe storms the beach is inundated and the breakers strike the dune line.

Your bike trip follows the main Refuge road. Park your car at parking lot 1 to your left after the Refuge entrance. All the trails are clearly marked. Before long you will leave the pavement and continue on gravel road. The board-walks to the beach are located at regular intervals, giving you an opportunity to view the river marshes along your way. There is an observation tower at parking lot 4 where you can climb up to get a better feel of your surroundings. Sandy Point State Reservation is the end of the road, at the tip of the island. Camping is allowed, and you'll find another observation tower there. The total distance round trip is about 13 miles.

Plum Island (continued)

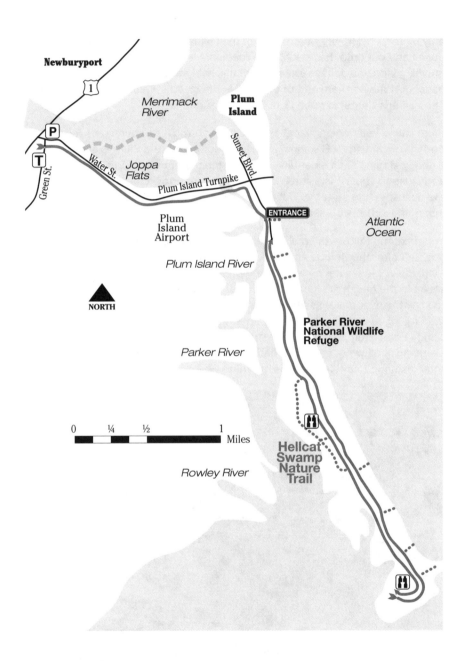

Newburyport

1

Merrimack River

Plum Island

P

T

Green St.

Water St.

Joppa Flats

Plum Island Turnpike

Sunset Blvd.

ENTRANCE

Plum Island Airport

Atlantic Ocean

Plum Island River

NORTH

Parker River

Parker River National Wildlife Refuge

0   ¼   ½   1
Miles

Hellcat Swamp Nature Trail

Rowley River

Province Lands Trail

Grid	CC
Length	7.5 miles
Surface	Paved
Setting	Relatively flat, beach front, ponds
Difficulty	Moderate
Vicinity	Provincetown
Lat/Long	42-04/70-13 Parking off Province Lands Road
County	Barnstable
Contact	Cape Cod National Seashore 99 Marconi Site Road Wellfleet, MA 02667 508-349-3785

Facilities

Getting There
Take Route 6 eastbound into Provincetown. At the first traffic light, turn right onto Race Point Road. Follow the road for about 1.5 miles to a large brown National Park Service sign on the right. Turn right at the sign into the parking lot by the Province Lands Visitor Center.

Trail Notes
The Province Lands Trail is located at the northern end of Cape Cod Historical Seashore, approximately 1-mile from Provincetown. The Visitor Center sits atop a sand dune 100 feet above sea level, providing a commanding view of the area with its 360-degree observation deck. Information and assistance is available from park rangers who staff the Visitor Center. It is open from May 1 through October, and from 9am to 5pm daily.

The Province Lands Bike Trail loop can be accessed from the Visitor Center. The loop is 5.3 miles around. By riding the trail spurs to Herring Cove Beach,

Province Lands Trail (continued)

Race Point Beach and Bennet Pond you can add another two miles to the ride. The trail is easy to moderate, and is scheduled for re-surfacing starting in 2008. The bike trail will be widened to a width of 10 feet, from the current 8 feet, except where it passes alongside wetland areas. The rehabilitation plans for the trail include retaining walls, slope stabilization plantings, a sand fence in places where the sand drifts across the trail, and some minor re-alignments. New signs, a centerline, and other pavement markings would also be added.

Access Points:

Beach Forest parking area

Province Lands Visitor Center

Race Point Beach parking area

Herring Cove Beach parking area

Race Point Road near Provincetown

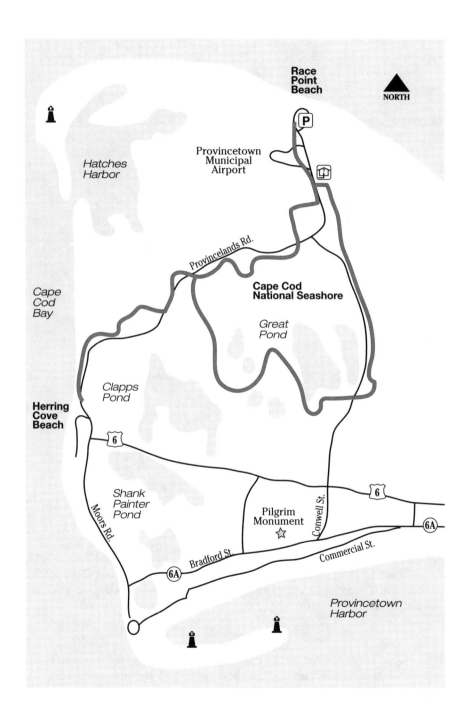

Race
Point
Beach

NORTH

Provincetown
Municipal
Airport

Hatches
Harbor

Provincelands Rd.

Cape Cod
National Seashore

Cape
Cod
Bay

Great
Pond

Clapps
Pond

Herring
Cove
Beach

6

Shank
Painter
Pond

Moors Rd.

Pilgrim
Monument

Conwell St.

6

6A

Bradford St.

6A

Commercial St.

Provincetown
Harbor

Ravenswood Park

Grid	C12
Length	10 miles
Surface	Singletrack, graveled carriage roads
Setting	Wooded flatlands, boulders, swamp, ocean views
Difficulty	Easy to moderate
Acres	600
Fees	Must be a Trustee member or obtain a mountain biking pass. Call 978-921-1944
Hours	Sunrise to Sunset – closed to mountain biking from March 1 through April 30.
Vicinity	Gloucester
Lat/Long	42-35/70-42 Hwy 127 & Old Salem Road
County	Essex
Contact	Ravenswood Park Beverly, MA 978-526-8687
Facilities	P

Getting There
Take Route 128 to Route 133 (Exit 14) and follow it east towards Gloucester for 3 miles to a "T" intersection with Route127 (Western Avenue). Take a right onto Route 127 for 2 miles to the park entrance, marked by a large sign. The parking area is on the right.

Trail Notes
Ravenswood Park is a nature reserve in the western section of Gloucester. In the late 19th century, Samuel Sawyer, a noted businessman and philan-

thropist, developed a plan to preserve the woods in Gloucester. Over the years he purchased woodlots, old pastures, and swampland near Freshwater Cove. At his death he left the land to a board of trustees with an endowment and instructions that it be turned into a park. Through the years the trustees continued to acquire adjacent parcels of land.

Ravenswood Park offers a tranquil wooded setting with almost ten miles of trail and carriage paths. The carriage roads are surfaced with a dense crushed stone, making for easy riding. The singletrack can be challenging and technical varying from rolling forestland to granite boulder fields with short climbs and descents. The singletrack begins close to the parking lot. These trails are only occasionally marked. Mountain biking is permitted only on designated trails from May 1 to February 28. Special attractions include an overlook to Gloucester harbor and a boardwalk through the Great Magnolia Swamp. A plaque marks the spot in the woods where Mason Walton, "The Hermit" built his cabin in the 1880's.

A popular recreational adventure is known as the "Quest". You are given clues and a map to follow to a hidden treasure box at the end of this Quest. There you can sign in, collect a copy of the Quest's stamp, and then replace the box for the next visitor.

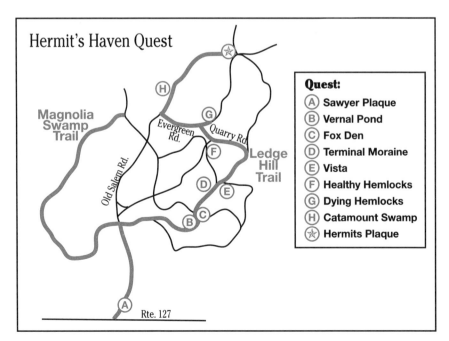

Ravenswood Park (continued)

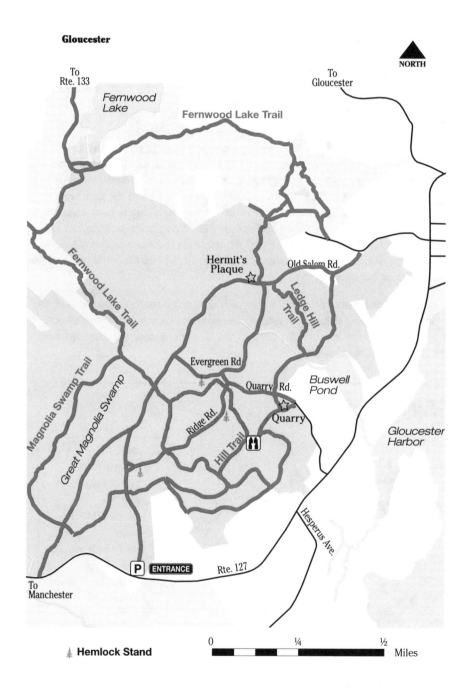

Gloucester

NORTH

To
Rte. 133

To
Gloucester

Fernwood
Lake

Fernwood Lake Trail

Fernwood Lake Trail

Hermit's
Plaque

Old Salem Rd.

Ledge Hill
Trail

Magnolia Swamp Trail

Great Magnolia Swamp

Evergreen Rd

Quarry Rd.

Buswell
Pond

Ridge Rd.

Hill Trail

Quarry

Gloucester
Harbor

Hesperus Ave.

P ENTRANCE Rte. 127

To
Manchester

🌲 **Hemlock Stand**

0   ¼   ½

Miles

Savoy Mountain State Forest

Grid	C2
Length	40 miles (plus 10 miles in Florida State Forest)
Surface	Dirt and gravel forest roads, doubletrack, some singletrack
Setting	Hardwood forests, ponds, hills and summits
Difficulty	Easy to moderate
Acres	11,118
Fees	Access is free, except parking at North Pond day-use area or the campground
Hours	8 am to dusk, year-round
Vicinity	Florida, North Adams
Lat/Long	42-37/43-02 Tanner & New State Road
County	Berkshire
Contact	Savoy Mountain State Forest 260 Central Shaft Road Florida, MA 01247 413-663-8469 Campground: 413-664-9567
Facilities	P 👫 🏕 🍴 ⛺

Getting There

From I-91: Take I-91 to Route 2 in Greenfield (Exit 26), and go west for 31.4 miles to the town of Florida. Turn left onto Central Shaft Road, and stay to the right at the next 2 forks. The park headquarters is 2.8 miles from Route 2, the North Pond day-use area is 3.3 miles, and the campground is 3.7 miles from Route 2.

From I-90: Take I-90 to Route 20 in Lee (Exit 2). Take Route 20 west to Route 7 north to Williamstown for 31.7 miles. From Williamstown take Route 2 east for 11.2 miles to downtown North Adams. Turn right on Central Shaft Road and stay to the right at the next 2 forks. The park headquarters is 2.8 miles from Route 2.

Trail Notes

Savoy Mountain State Forest is located atop the Hoosac Mountain Range in northwestern Massachusetts. "Hoosac" is an Algonquin word meaning "place of stones". Apple trees interspersed throughout the campground and stonewalls are some reminders of the area's once farming history. The Interpretive Center offers guided hikes and slideshows. The campground, located at South Pond, provides flush toilets and showers. In addition, the scenic North and South Ponds, framed by woods with hills rising in the distance, offer picnicking, swimming and fishing opportunities. Try to visit Tannery Falls and nearby Parker Brook Falls, where Ross Brook flows through a deep chasm before cascading over 50 feet to a clear pool below. You can also hike the Bog Pond Trail, with its floating bog islands, or climb Spruce Hill on the Busby Trail for some breathtaking views. Borden Mountain rises to 2,500 feet about sea level, and is topped by a fire tower. It's a long climb but the view is breathtaking. Motorized vehicles are prohibited, as well as swimming or climbing at the Tannery Falls area.

Most of the roads in the forest are open to mountain biking. These wooded trails consist of a mix of rolling dirt roads, rugged four-wheel trails, and singletrack through roots, rocks, mud holes, and hairpin turns. Before starting your ride, stop at the Ranger Station for a detailed map and current trail conditions. This is a remote area, so be prepared for the unexpected. There are many access points, but a suggested place to start is from the parking area on Burnett Road. The loop options take advantage of combinations of trails such as Tannery Road, Balance Rock Trail, Lewis Trail, and Fire Tower Trails. From Tannery Road you can get to one of the two "Balanced Rocks" by taking a series of steep switchbacks. Get to the second one by taking the easier "Loop Trail" located by South Pond. Tannery Falls can be accessed from Tannery Road, but it's limited to hiking.

Trails

1. Lost Pond Trail
2. Busby Trail
3. Blackburnian Loop
4. North Pond Loop
5. D. Poland Loop
6. Flat Rock Hill Trail
7. South Pond Loop
8. Haskins Rail
9. Bog Pond Trail
10. Tyler Swamp Loop
11. Florida Trail
12. Adams Sno-drifters Trail
13. Sucker Brook Trail
14. Carpenter Trail
15. Shaker Trail
16. Tannery Trail
17. Burnett Pond Trail
18. Ross Brook Trail
19. H.H. Fitzroy Trail
20. Hamlet Trail
21. Lewis Hill Trail
22. Balance Rock Trail
23. C. C. Trail
24. Fire Tower Trail
25. Kamick Trail
26. Savoy Kanary Kats Trail
27. Hathaway Trail
28. Tilton Brook Trail

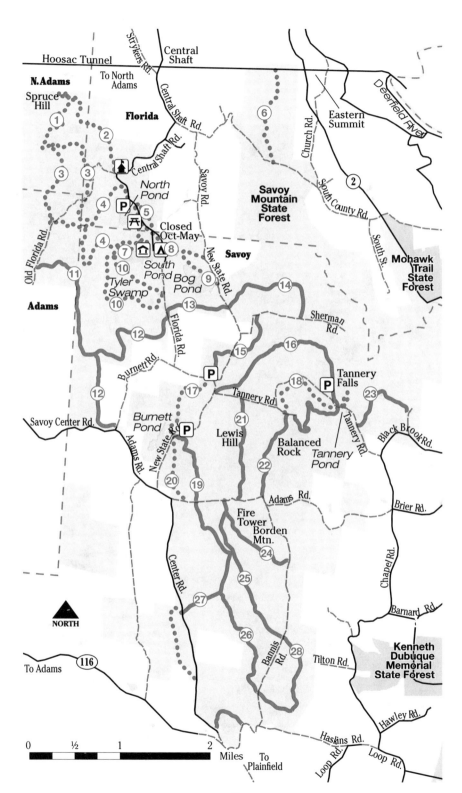

Hoosac Tunnel

Central
Shaft

N. Adams

Spruce
Hill

To North
Adams

Florida

Strykers Rd.

Central Shaft Rd.

Central Shaft Rd.

North
Pond

P

Closed
Oct-May

Savoy Rd.

Savoy
Mountain
State
Forest

Church Rd.

Eastern
Summit

Deerfield River

2

South County Rd.

South St.

Mohawk
Trail
State
Forest

Savoy

South
Pond

Tyler
Swamp

Bog
Pond

New State Rd.

Adams

Old Florida Rd.

Florida Rd.

Sherman
Rd.

Burnett Rd.

Tannery
Falls

P

Tannery Rd.

Burnett
Pond

P

Lewis
Hill

Balanced
Rock

Tannery
Pond

Tannery Rd.

Black Brook Rd.

Savoy Center Rd.

New State Rd.

Adams Rd.

Adams Rd.

Fire
Tower
Borden
Mtn.

Brier Rd.

Chapel Rd.

Center Rd.

Barnard Rd.

NORTH

Kenneth
Dubuque
Memorial
State Forest

116

To Adams

Bannis Rd.

Tilton Rd.

0   ½   1   2
Miles

To
Plainfield

Haskins Rd.

Hawley Rd.

Loop Rd.

Loop Rd.

Savoy Mountain State Forest

Courtesy of the Massachusetts Department of Conservation & Recreation. Photo by Kandra Clineff for the DCR©

154

Stony Brook Reservation

Grid	D10
Length	12 miles
Surface	Paved, natural
Setting	Tree covered hills, valleys, wetlands, rock outcroppings
Difficulty	Easy to moderate
Acres	475
Hours	Dawn to dusk, year round
Vicinity	Hyde Park, West Roxbury
Lat/Long	42-15/71-08 Connell Field area off Turtle Pond Parkway
County	Suffolk
Contact	Stony Brook Reservation Turtle Pond Parkway West Roxbury, Hyde Park, MA 01236 617-698-1802
Facilities	

Getting There
From Washington Street at Forest Hills Station, go 3 miles on Washington Street towards Dedham, and then turn left onto Turtle Pond Parkway.

To get there using the MBTA, take the Orange line to Forest Hills Station, then the Dedham bus to Turtle Pond Parkway.

Trail Notes
Stony Brook Reservation contains 475-acres of scenic landscapes and a variety of recreational facilities in the southern section, including a pool, picnic area, an ice skating rink, bathhouses, fishing, a butterfly garden, and the John F. Thompson Center. It is maintained by the Department of Conservation and

Recreation. Stony Brook is the former site of a sawmill, and has an extensive boardwalk between Kingfisher Pond and Teal Marsh, ending near a waterfall.

There are some 12 miles of bicycle paths and hiking trails that meander through the quiet, forested portion of the reservation, taking you through tree covered hills, valleys, rock outcroppings and wetland, past Turtle Pond and into Hyde Park. Mountain biking is allowed on established trails from April 15 through December 31.

The largest and most accessible portion of the park can be reached from a small paved parking lot just east of the intersection of the Enneking, Dedham, and Turtle Pond Parkways. There is a paved pathway that loops around most of the perimeter. There are also dirt paths that lead to Turtle Pond or the quieter inner portion of the park.

Trails

1. Wood Path
2. East Boundary Path
3. Bearberry Hill Path
4. Lawrence Path
5. Johnson Path
6. Turtle Pond Path
7. Gabreski Path
8. McGuire Path
9. Evans Path
10. Winchester Path
11. Stony Brook Path
12. Adams Path
13. Hull Path
14. Lee Path
15. Stewart Path
16. Overbrook Path
17. Gavin Path
18. Meyer Path
19. Otis Path
20. Knox Path
21. Bold Knob Path
22. Chamberlain Path
23. Smith Path
24. Bufford Path
25. Sells Path
26. Rooney Rock Path

DCR Visitor Guidelines
- The park is open dawn to dusk
- Dogs must be leashed and waste removed
- Mountain biking allowed on established trails from April 15 to December 31
- Visitors must abide by park signage

The following is prohibited
- Motorized vehicles
- Hunting or trapping
- Fires
- Alcoholic beverages
- Removal of any park resource
  Failure to comply may result in arrest and/or fine per order of MGLC 92, S.37

Important Contacts
- Emergency: 911
- 24 Hour DCR Radio Dispatch: 617-722-1188
- State Police: 617-698-5840

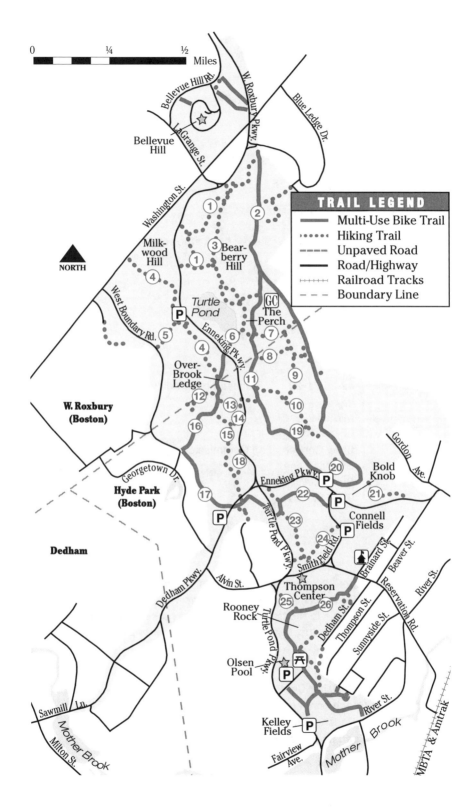

TRAIL LEGEND

▬▬▬	Multi-Use Bike Trail
••••••	Hiking Trail
– – –	Unpaved Road
▬▬▬	Road/Highway
┼┼┼┼┼	Railroad Tracks
– – –	Boundary Line

Bellevue Hill Rd.

W. Roxbury Pkwy.

Blue Ledge Dr.

Miles

0   ¼   ½

NORTH

Bellevue Hill

LaGrange St.

Washington St.

Milk-wood Hill

Bearberry Hill

West Boundary Rd.

Turtle Pond

Enneking Pkwy.

Over-Brook Ledge

GC
The Perch

W. Roxbury (Boston)

Georgetown Dr.

Hyde Park (Boston)

Dedham

Enneking Pkwy.

Bold Knob

Gordon Ave.

Connell Fields

Turtle Pond Pkwy.

Smith Field Rd.

Brainard St.

Beaver St.

Dedham Pkwy.

Alvin St.

Thompson Center

Rooney Rock

Thompson St.

Dedham St.

Sunnyside St.

Reservation Rd.

River St.

Olsen Pool

Turtle Pond Pkwy.

Sawmill Ln.

Milton St.

Mother Brook

Kelley Fields

Fairview Ave.

River St.

Mother Brook

MBTA & Amtrak

157

Stow Town Forest

Grid	D9
Length	12 miles
Surface	Singletrack. Dirt roads
Setting	Woodlands, wetlands, flat & smooth doubletrack, twisty singletrack
Difficulty	Easy to moderate
Acres	360
Vicinity	Stow
Lat/Long	42-26/71-29 Trailhead off Bradley Lane
County	Middlesex
Contact	Stow Conservation Commission Bradley Lane Stow, MA 978-897-8615
Facilities	

Getting There

Stow is located about 20 miles west of Boston. From the junction of Routes 117 and 62, take Route 117 west to Bradley Lane in Stow, then south to its end for less than a mile to the trailhead. The large parking lot, which also serves nearby playing fields, is just west of the Stow Shopping Center.

Trail Access Points:
Beech Forest parking area
Province Lands Visitor Center
Race Point Beach parking area
Herring Cove Beach parking area
Race Point Road near Provincetown

Trail Notes

Stow Town Forest, also known as Gardner Hill Town Forest Conservation Area offers over 360 acres of densely wooded forest. It's secluded and usually quite quiet. The town forest encompasses tree-topped Gardner Hill, gravel pits, and a stretch of the north shore of the Assabet River. The trails consist of old woods roads, most of which are smooth and flat. Trail users must stay on the marked trail system. They loop around the forest with few hills. Most of the singletrack trails travel on sand and gravel. They are pretty much rock free, but there are plenty of roots to contend with as you ride through the woods on fairly flat terrain. There are some steep hills, sharp turns and low areas subject to flooding. Near the Assabet River you'll follow the low ridgelines and around the sandy drumlins.

Horseback riding, camping, snowmobiling, and night use is allowed by permit only. Fishing is allowed in the Assabet River and Elizabeth Brook. While picnicking is allowed, there are no refuse containers so everything that is carried in must be carried out. You might be wise to bring insect repellent when conditions are hot or wet.

This is a quick trail guide as suggested by the Stow Conservation Trust:

1. From Bradley Lane trailhead, follow red trail across footbridge, bearing right at Y-junction with blue.

2. Continue on red to range, left on orange.

3. Follow orange to white, right on white.

4. Follow white to yellow, left on yellow.

5. Follow yellow to next trail on right, turn right (unblazed).

6. Follow unblazed trail to and alongside river to T-junction with yellow, right on yellow.

7. Follow yellow to 4-way junction, straight on unblazed trail parallel to river.

8. Follow unblazed trail up and down, often steeply, as long as you care to, then return to junction with yellow, turn right on yellow.

(Continued on following page)

9. Take next unblazed trail to left and up Gardner Hill, past junction with white trail to right.

10. Turn right at next trail junction, continuing uphill toward summit.

11. Near summit, turn right to return downhill.

12. At the next junction, turn right on the white-blazed trail.

13. Turn left at T-junction to continue on white.

14. Bear left on the very wide blue-blazed track.

15. Follow blue to Y-junction with red; bear right on red across foot-bridge to return to parking area.

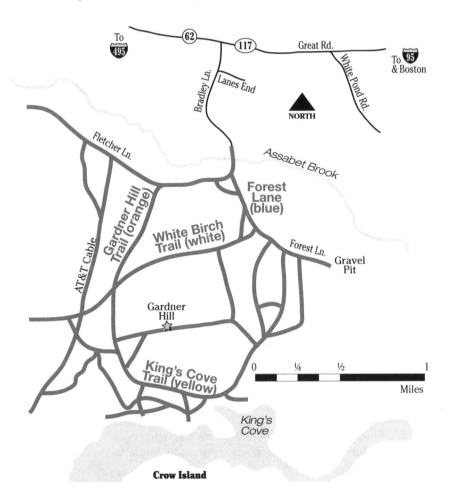

Upton State Forest

Grid	E6
Length	15 miles
Surface	Singletrack, fire roads
Setting	Thick woodland, marshland, boulders
Difficulty	Easy to difficult
Acres	2,660
Hours	Dawn to dusk
Vicinity	Upton
Lat/Long	42-13/71-37 Westboro & Southboro Road
County	Worcester
Contact	Hopkinson State Park 508-435-4303
	Visitor's Center 508-278-7604
Facilities	

Getting There
From Boston, take I-90 east to I-495 (Exit 21B), then south to Route 135. Take Route 135 west for 3.5 miles to Westboro Road, then south (left) for about 2 miles to Spring Street. Turn right a very short distance further to a fire road that takes you to the parking area.

Trail Notes
Upton State Forest is located in the southeastern part of central Massachusetts in the Blackstone River Valley. Its 2,660 acres are scattered through Upton and extend into the surrounding towns. Before the arrival of European settlers Upton was a pass through place for Native Americans. There is no

Upton State Forest (continued)

evidence of permanent occupation and, except for travel between villages or hunting, this area belonged to the wildlife. The headquarters area and parking lot for the major trails are located near the intersection of Westborough and Southborough Roads in Upton. The thick woodland is laced with boulders and low-lying marshland. Hunting is permitted in season.

The trails are generally well marked and maintained, and are applicable to all skill levels. They are easy to follow and getting lost should not be a problem. You can take moderate loops by using the wider, graveled jeep roads, or the more rugged double track trails. There are a lot of short climbs and descents, but not too many big hills. Rabbit Run Trail will give you a good start. The Mammoth Rock Trail takes you between boulders as you pass through flat and thickly wooded forest. The ride up the Grouse, Mammoth Rock and Whistling Cave trails can be a real challenge. They are mostly all singletrack with a bunch of tough sections. Another suggested ride is the Peppercorn Hill area. The hill is steep and tough climbing, but the downhill is great. Your ride through Upton State Forest will include narrow twisting trails, thick woodland laced with boulders, marshland, and a overhead canopy of tall white pines.

TRAIL LEGEND

————	Multi-Use Bike Trail
————	Paved Road
--------	Unpaved Road
————	Road/Highway
·•·•·•·•·	Power Line
– – – – –	Boundary Line

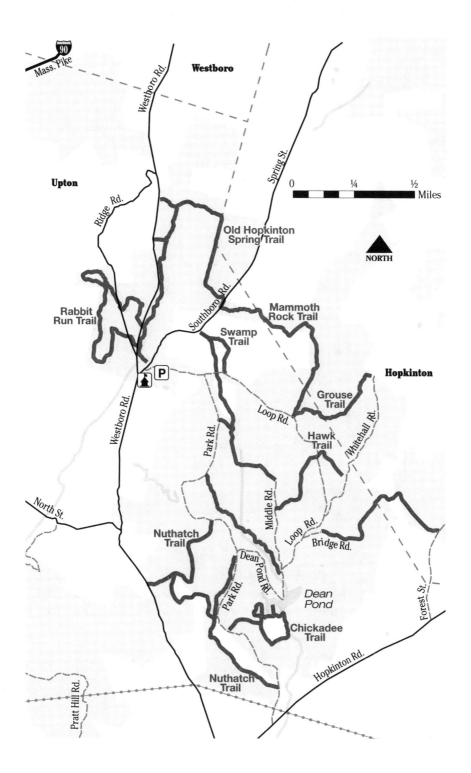

Willowdale State Forest

Grid	C11
Length	40 miles
Surface	Doubletrack, singletrack, dirt roads
Setting	Dense woods, flat & smooth doubletrack to twisty singletrack
Difficulty	Easy to moderate
Acres	2,400
Hours	Dawn to dusk
Vicinity	Ipswich
Lat/Long	42-40/70-54 Entrance off Topsfield Road
County	Essex
Contact	Bradley Palmer State Park Linebrook Road Ipswich, MA 978-887-5931
Facilities	P

Getting There
From Boston, take I-95 to Route 1 (Exit 50). Go north on Route 1 for 4 miles to Ipswich Road. Take a right on Ipswich Road for about 2 miles to the park entrance. The trail is marked with a signpost. Ipswich Road turns into Topsfield Road in Ipswich.

Additional parking:
At an old road bed at Route 1 and West Street
The trail crossing at Old Right Road
The trail crossing at Linebrook Road near Hood Pond

Trail Notes

Willowdale State Forest is located in northeastern Massachusetts, between Bradley Palmer State Park and Georgetown-Rowley State Forest. "Willow Dale" was once part of Bradley Palmer's 10,000-acre North Shore Estate. There are no developed facilities at the Forest. It consists of two separate parcels divided by Route 1. The eastern block abuts Bradley Palmer State Park and the Ipswich River. The Pine Swamp area is to the east of Route 1 and the Hood Pond/Cleveland Farm area is to the west. The Hood Pond section contains woodlands, streams, and lakeshore with swamplands surrounding the east end. The terrain consists of maintained dirt roads, doubletrack and singletrack. The doubletrack is mostly smooth running, but the singletrack can be tight and twisty. The low-lying sections often become muddy and slick after heavy rains. Be aware that hunting is permitted in season (November and December).

There are roughly 40 miles of trail, but the main routes are blazed in red and blue, combining to make a 7 mile loop through thick forest of maple, oak, and white pine. While most of this route is wide, smooth doubletrack, there are some challenging singletrack sections combining roots, rocks and other obstacles.

The Bay Circuit Trail leaves the Pine Swamp section at West Street in Ipswich. You can park on the east side of Route 1 on the old roadbed. To continue on to the Hood Pond section, cross Route 1 heading west, but use caution crossing. Shortly after passing by an industrial building, the trail bears left off of the larger trail and heads southwest past the houses and pastures to your right. The trail continues past a marsh and ponds on the left, and then crosses a stone wall, turning right at the top of a small hill as you head northwest.

	TRAIL LEGEND
▬▬▬▬▬	Trail
⋈ ⋈ ⋈ ⋈ ⋈ ⋈ ⋈	Bay Circuit Trail
▬ ▬ ▬ ▬ ▬ ▬ ▬	Unpaved Road
▬▬▬▬▬	Road/Highway
- - - - - -	Boundary Line

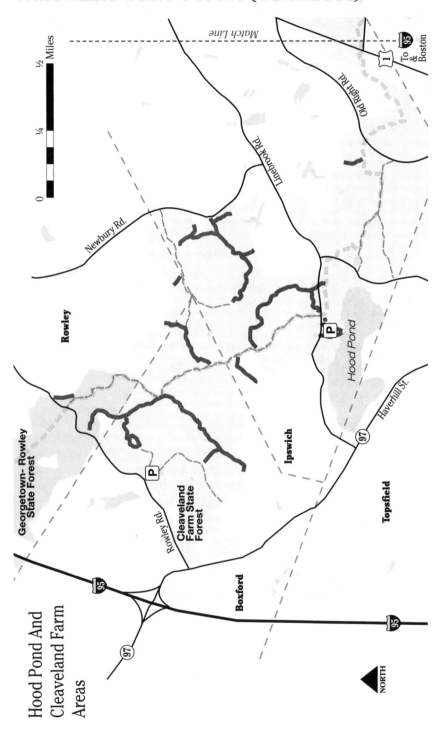

Hood Pond And Cleaveland Farm Areas

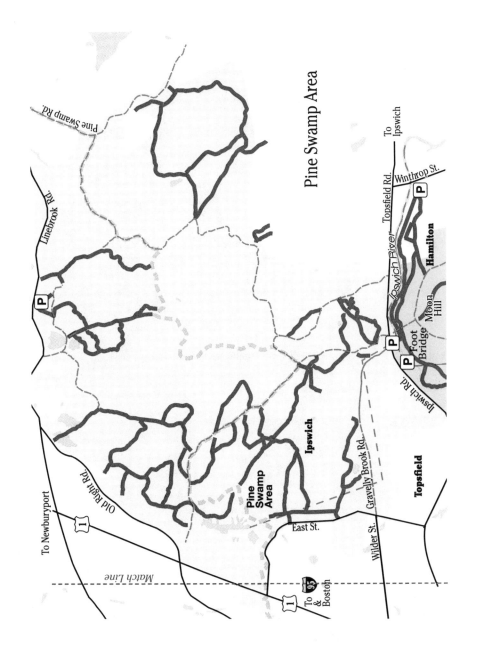

Pine Swamp Area

Windsor State Forest

Grid	C3
Length	15 miles
Surface	Dirt roads, singletrack
Setting	Mixed woods, meadow bottoms, rocky gorge of Windsor Jambs
Difficulty	Easy to moderate
Acres	1,740
Fees	Vehicle entry for the day use area, from May through Labor Day
Hours	Sunrise to sunset, year round
Vicinity	Windsor
Lat/Long	42-31/72-60 Trailhead at River & Lower Road
County	Berkshire
Contact	Windsor State Forest River Road Windsor, MA 413-684-0948 413-268-7098 (off-season)
Facilities	

Getting There

From the East: Take I-90 to I-91 in West Springfield (Exit 4). Proceed north to Route 9 in Northampton (Exit 19). Go west on Route 9 for 27.8 miles to West Cummington. Turn right onto West Main Street for 0.1 mile, then left onto River Road for 2.9 miles to the day-use area entrance on the left. The campground is on the right.

From the West: At the intersection of Route 9 and Route 8 in Dalton, take
Route 9 east for 11.3 miles to West Cummington. Turn left onto West Main
Street for 0.1 mile, then left onto River Road for 2.9 miles to the day-use area
entrance on the left.

Trail Notes

Windsor State Forest is located in the northern part of the Berkshires in
western Massachusetts, about 20 miles northeast of Pittsfield. Facilities at
the popular day-use area include a sandy swimming beach and picnic areas.
There are also limited-service campsites (no showers or flush toilets). A
highlight of the forest is the cascading waterfall at Windsor Jambs. Windsor
Jambs Brook plunges through a 25-foot-wide gorge, with 80-foot-high granite
walls on either side. Located deep in the rolling hills the falls stand out for its
spectacular beauty and as a refreshing place to visit.

The trial terrain varies between narrow dirt roads, rugged jeep roads and
some singletrack. Start your ride from the swimming beach parking area
on Lower Road, crossing an intersection and then right at the intersection.
You will pass scenic Windsor Jambs waterfalls on the right. Further, the trail
becomes more rugged and downhill until you come out on a narrow dirt road.
Take two lefts to reach a three-way intersection. Turn left again to come back
to the intersection passed before Windsor Jambs. Just keep going straight to
return to the swimming beach. As an alternative, your ride can be lengthened
by turning right at the intersection and, with a map in hand, explore the other
loop options.

TRAIL LEGEND	
═══════════	Trail
───────────	Paved Road
▪▪▪▪▪▪▪▪▪▪	Unpaved Road
▬▬▬▬▬▬▬▬	Road/Highway
┼┼┼┼┼┼┼┼┼┼	Railroad Tracks
─ ─ ─ ─ ─ ─	Boundary Line

Windsor State Forest (continued)

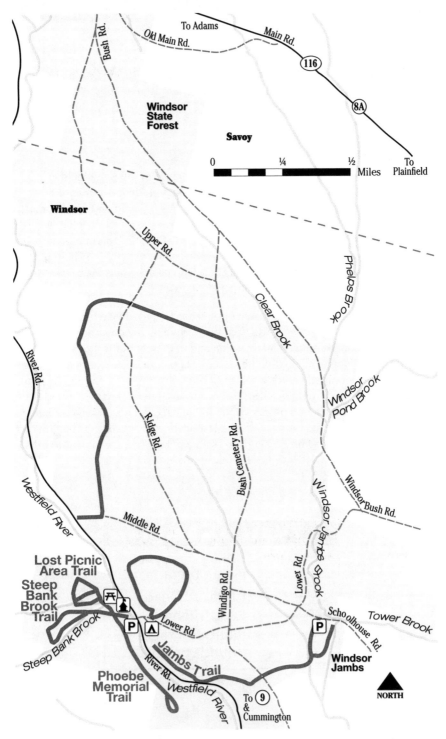

Wompatuck State Park

Grid	E11
Length	12 miles paved, over 30 miles of mountain bike trail
Surface	Paved, bridle path, fire roads, singletrack
Setting	Woods, hills, sandy areas
Difficulty	Easy to moderate
Acres	3,500
Hours	Park – Dawn to dusk, campground office 8am to 10pm
Vicinity	Hingham
Lat/Long	42-12/70-51 Trailhead at Union Street
County	Plymouth
Contact	Wompatuck State Park Union Street Hingham, MA 781-749-7160
Facilities	

Getting There
From the North (Boston): Take I-93 South to Route 3, then south to Route 228 (Exit 14). Follow Route 228 North for about 5 miles to the intersection with Free Street on the right. Turn right on Free Street for 1 mile to the park entrance on the right. The camping area is 1.5 miles into the park on the right.

From the South and Cape Cod: Take Route 3 North to Route 228 (Exit 14). Follow Route 228 North for about 5 miles to Free Street on the right. Turn right on Free Street for 1 mile to the park entrance on the right.

Wompatuck State Park (continued)

Trail Notes

Wompatuck State Park is located near Hingham on Boston's South Shore. The park and surrounding lands were deeded by an Indian chief known as Josiah Wompatuck in 1665, after whom the park was named. This is a wooded landscape of oaks and evergreens, ponds, and old stone walls. A notable feature of the park is Mount Blue Spring, which is a fresh source of drinking water for visitors. Facilities include 280 campsites with electrical and water hookups, restrooms, and picnic areas. The park is popular with trailer campers. A boat ramp is provided for car-top boats. In addition to riding the 12-mile paved trail, there are many miles of flat paved roads that are not open to automobiles.

There are over 30-miles of multi-loop trails on a combination of double track, single track, packed dirt and paved park roads. Effort level is moderate with frequent roots, rocks, and sandy areas. Some of the singletrack is fast while others are like constantly turning long distance runs. Logs and rocks are a frequent challenge. Prospect Hill is the highest hill in the park with multiple routes to the top, several of which are singletrack. The trails are generally marked with arrows and signs or orange paint splotches and streamers. Wompatuck is host to a mountain bike race each year in June sponsored by NEMBA. NEMBA has been active in supporting trail maintenance, such as building bridges and erosion control.

TRAIL LEGEND	
━━━━━━	Paved Trail
▪▪▪▪▪▪▪▪	Trail
──────	Paved Road closed to motorized traffic
━━━━━━	Road/Highway
·•·•·•·•·	Power/Pipe Line
– – – – –	Boundary Line

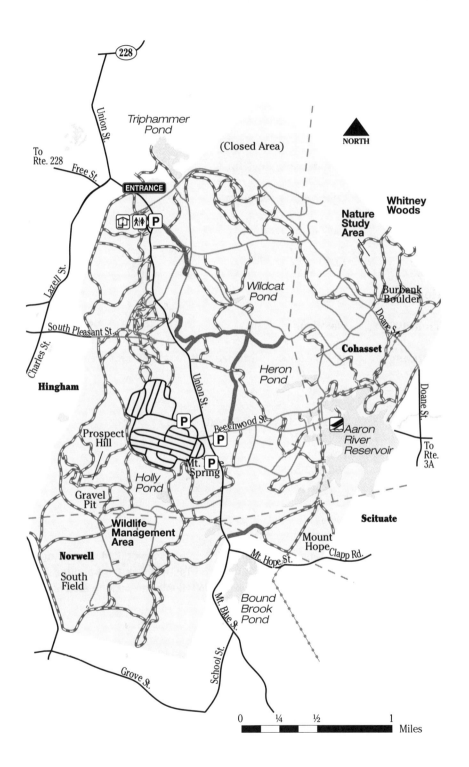

228

Triphammer
Pond

(Closed Area)

NORTH

To
Rte. 228 Free St.

Union St.

ENTRANCE

Whitney
Woods

Nature
Study
Area

Lazell St.

Wildcat
Pond

Burbank
Boulder

South Pleasant St.

Charles St.

Cohasset

Doane St.

Hingham

Heron
Pond

Union St.

P

Beechwood St.

Prospect
Hill

P

P

Aaron
River
Reservoir

Doane St.

To
Rte.
3A

Mt.
Spring

P

Holly
Pond

Gravel
Pit

Wildlife
Management
Area

Scituate

Norwell

South
Field

Mount
Hope

Clapp Rd.

Mt. Hope St.

Mt. Blue St.

Bound
Brook
Pond

Grove St.

School St.

0   ¼   ½   1
Miles

Wrentham State Forest

Grid	E9
Length	30 miles
Surface	Forest roads, singletrack
Setting	Deep woods, rocky areas
Difficulty	Easy to moderate
Acres	1,060
Hours	Dawn to dusk
Vicinity	Wrentham
Lat/Long	41-02/72-19 Trailhead off Taunton Street
County	Norfolk
Contact	F. Gilbert Hills State Forest Mill Street Foxboro, MA 508-543-5850
Facilities	P

Getting There
From I-495 take US 1 south (Exit 14B) for 0.6 miles to a stoplight. Take a right onto Taunton Street (Route 152). Continue on Taunton Street for another 0.6 miles. After crossing a bridge over I-495, turn left into the parking area and trailhead in the center of the forest..

Trail Notes
Wrentham State Forest is located in southeastern Massachusetts just south of the town of Wrentham, and about 30 miles southwest of Boston. It is part of the F. Gilbert Hills State Forest, and connects to the Foxboro State Forest. There are miles and miles of trails, many not marked, but you are never far from one of the four paved roads that surround the forest - I-495, Taunton

Street, Hwy I-40, and Madison Street. The landscape is a mix including red pine, spruce, oak, maple, and blueberry bushes, as well as some imposing granite outcroppings. Quail, turkeys, and pheasants are common. There is no campground. Hunting is allowed in season. Most of the trails are well drained and rolling, with a lot of short, steep climbs and descents. Loose scrabble and sandy areas are not uncommon.

The forest is divided into three sections by I-495 and Taunton Street. The eastern section is the area with the most trails and deepest woods. The suggested starting point is the trailhead from the parking lot off Taunton Street. Cross the street and turn left to a fire gate a short distance further. Go through the gate and start climbing to where you can pick up one of several singletrack trails coming down the south and east side of the hill. If you are a newcomer to the area you might want enter the woods behind the lot and ride the trails closest to the highway fence as you travel, keeping the traffic to your left. If you continue as far as Hwy 1A you are at the edge of the forest. Another route is to start out on one of the fire roads heading east or west in the southern part of the forest. These fire roads in turn will lead you to a variety of trails that run through the towns of Plainfield, Atteborough, North Attleborough and eventually even into Rhode Island. There is also a marked loop that winds through this section.

TRAIL LEGEND	
▬▬▬▬▬	Multi-Use Bike Trail (non-motorized)
▪ ▬ ▬ ▬ ▬ ▬ ▬	Warner Trail
▪▪▪▪▪▪▪▪▪	Multi-Use Trail (motorized)
▬ ▬ ▬ ▬ ▬ ▬	Unpaved Road
▬▬▬▬▬▬▬	Road/Highway
– – – – – –	Boundary Line

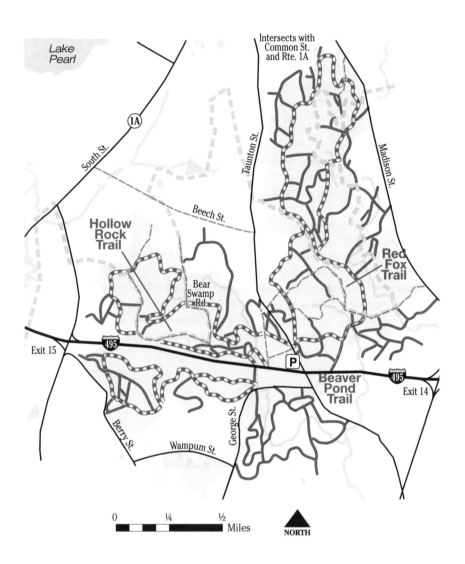

Yokun Ridge North (Burbank Trail)

Grid	D1
Length	5.2 miles
Surface	Doubletrack, singletrack, paved road
Setting	Rolling hills, winding loops
Difficulty	Moderate to difficult
Acres	407
Hours	Dawn to dusk
Vicinity	Lenox
Lat/Long	42-21/73-20 Trailhead area
County	Berkshire
Contact	Berkshire Natural Resources Council 20 Bank Row Pittsfield, MA 01201 413-499-0596
Facilities	P

Getting There

From the intersection Routes 7A and 183, go west on Route 183 for 1.5-miles to Richmond-Lenox Road, then right for 1.5-miles to a parking area on the left at Olivia's Overlook. This is a lookout above Stockbridge Bowl. The Burbank Trail is across the road.

Trail Notes

Located in the Berkshires on the southern slope of Lenox Mountain. The ride takes into beautiful woods, a quiet pond, an old farmhouse site, and several streams. The land and reservoir was once owned by Andrew Carnegie, and then occupied until 1970 by the Jesuits, where it became known as Monks

Yokun Ridge North – Burbank Trail (continued)

Pond. In 1998 the trail was dedicated to Kelton Burbank, a longtime friend of the Berkshire Natural Resources Council, managers of the property. The Council is a non-profit land conservation organization that has completed over 200 conservation projects encompassing 14,500 acres of conserved land throughout Berkshire County.

This is a place for peace and quiet and some challenging rides. The single-track offers plenty of tight turns, rolling terrain, and a long climb. The trail route consists of almost 3 miles of doubletrack, 2 miles of singletrack, and a half-mile of paved road. Burbank Trail provides a variety of biking options. You can follow the red blazed path right to Monks Pond or go left and up onto the ridge. Both trails join Old Baldhead Road to complete the route. From Monks Pond you can cross the dam, turning left onto Old Baldhead Road, or you can continue northeast on the western side of the pond. Both routes lead you to a junction north of the pond where you'll find the remains of the 1850's Gorman homestead. From there follow the red oval blaze to the top of the western ridge, where there is a scenic lookout. Continue southwest on the ridge to exit opposite Olivia's Overlook.

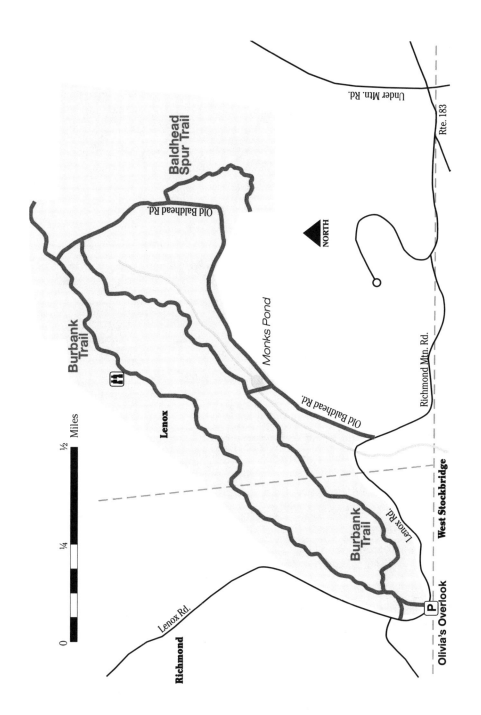

Baldhead
Spur Trail

Old Baldhead Rd.

Burbank
Trail

Lenox

Monks Pond

Old Baldhead Rd.

Burbank
Trail

Lenox Rd.

Richmond Mtn. Rd.

West Stockbridge

Olivia's Overlook

P

Lenox Rd.

Richmond

Under Mtn. Rd.

Rte. 183

NORTH

Miles

0   ¼   ½

Trail Index

MA Surfaced Trails

MA Mountain Biking Trails

City to Trail Index

City to Trail Index (continued)

Population Codes:

①	Up to 1,000
②	1,000 to 5,000
③	5,000 to 10,000
④	10,000 to 50,000
⑤	Over 50,000

County to Trail Index

County to Trail Index (continued)

Find me a place, safe and serene,

away from the terror I see on the screen.

A place where my soul can find some peace,

away from the stress and the pressures released.

A corridor of green not far from my home

for fresh air and exercise, quiet will roam.

Summer has smells that tickle my nose

and fall has the leaves that crunch under my toes.

Beware, comes a person we pass in a while

with a wave and hello and a wide friendly smile.

Recreation trails are the place to be,

to find that safe haven of peace and serenity.

By Beverly Moore, Illinois Trails Conservancy

American Bike Trails

publishes and distributes
maps, books and guides for the bicyclist.

For more information:
www.abtrails.com